The Warehouse Revolution

The Warehouse Revolution

Automate or Terminate

Peter Devenyi, Miguel Pinilla, and Jim Stollberg

BEP
BUSINESS EXPERT PRESS
Leader in applied, concise business books

The Warehouse Revolution: Automate or Terminate

First published in 2024 by
Business Expert Press, LLC
222 East 46th Street, New York, NY 10017
www.businessexpertpress.com

ISBN-13: 978-1-63742-573-2 (paperback)
ISBN-13: 978-1-63742-574-9 (e-book)

Business Expert Press Supply and Operations Management Collection

First edition: 2024

10 9 8 7 6 5 4 3 2 1

To my wife Sue, and my kids, Brittany, Josh, and Cassie, for all the love, support, and encouragement you have provided me throughout my career.
Peter Devenyi

To my wife Pam, daughter Marta, and son Pablo for a full life that made pursuing my career rewarding and fun. I would not be the person I am without you.
Miguel Pinilla

To my wife Leslie, son Justin, and daughter Lauren, for thriving through my absence while I globe trotted through my career. You are a blessing to me.
Jim Stollberg

Description

The *Warehouse Revolution* is a must-read for technologists, retailers, and investors who seek to understand the warehouse automation industry and the associated technologies. It walks through an array of automation options using understandable terms. It describes the history of the industry and how e-commerce catapulted warehouse automation to the forefront of supply chain operations. The book describes all associated processes including receiving, storage, picking, packing, sortation, and shipping. It compares manual, automated, and robotic alternatives in each case, highlighting the pros and cons. It will also be interesting to those who are simply curious and seek to understand what's happening behind the curtain: the highly choreographed movement of people and machines that enable packages to show up at our respective doorsteps in less than a day.

Keywords

warehouse automation; distribution center; fulfillment center; e-commerce fulfillment; robotics; articulated arm robot; automated storage and retrieval system; ASRS; shuttle system; cubic storage system; autonomous mobile robot; AMR; warehouse execution system; WES; warehouse control system; WCS; automated guided vehicle; AGV; industrial automation; microfulfillment center; storage system; picking; packing; shipping; receiving; sortation; linear sorter; crossbelt sorter; circular sorter; conveyor; warehouse management system; WMS; artificial intelligence; goods-to-person; person-to-goods; supply chain management

Contents

Testimonials

"The Warehouse Revolution is a must read for anyone who has an interest in the rapidly evolving warehouse automation industry. The authors, all veteran industry experts, have written a comprehensive, easy to read, and very interesting history of this industry, which has evolved from being a mere cost center to being a critical element of competitiveness in many industries."
—Rick Wagoner, Retired CEO, General Motors

"The Warehouse Revolution offers a comprehensive and easy-to-read account of the past, present, and future of the warehousing industry and all associated technologies. It should serve as a launch pad for anyone who is new to the industry or for those who are facing automation investment decisions in the coming years. With unprecedented market growth levels anticipated over the course of the next decade, this book couldn't have come at a better time!"—**Jeff Moss, CEO, Ascential Technologies**

"I would highly recommend this book to anyone interested in warehouse automation. It provides a comprehensive overview of the topic, including the latest technologies and trends. The authors draw from their extensive experience and deep knowledge of both the industry and the science to provide an excellent explanation of the benefits of warehouse automation and how it can help businesses improve efficiency and competitiveness. I particularly enjoyed the sections on software and the future evolution of the industry, with artificial intelligence and robotics being two of the most promising technologies for warehouse automation. Overall, this is an essential read for anyone who wants to stay ahead of the curve in the ever-changing world of logistics."—**Dr. Eike Boehm, Retired CTO, KION Group**

Acknowledgments

We would like to express our gratitude to the team at Business Expert Press, in particular to Scott Isenberg, Joy Field, and Charlene Kronstedt for their input and assistance, and for the faith they showed in us writing this book. They recognized that it would help plug a hole in previously available Supply Chain literature.

The Exeter Premedia Services team made the copyedit process as painless as possible for us. They skillfully and efficiently addressed numerous issues in our manuscript and ensured the book was fully compliant with BEP standards.

We would also like to thank all the companies that generously contributed photos for this book including AutoStore, Brightpick, Clear-Path Robotics, Covariant, Dematic, Exotec, Hai Robotics, Matthews Automation Solutions, Reel-in Robotics, and Tompkins Robotics. We appreciate your support very much.

Finally, we have to acknowledge the generous mentors and talented colleagues we worked with over the years. While there are too many of you to mention by name, you inspired us immensely. We would not have been able to write this book were it not for your many contributions in advancing the field of warehouse automation over the past 20 years.

—Pete Devenyi, Miguel Pinilla, Jim Stollberg

Introduction

A good friend of ours, a self-proclaimed coffee aficionado, recently purchased an espresso machine on Amazon. It was one of those high-end models that grinds the beans, adjusts the strength, and warms the milk, all with the touch of a button. He clicked the order button at 8 am and by 4 pm, much to his delight, the 40-pound wonder-machine was sitting on his doorstep.

While most of us could not imagine such possibilities a decade ago, it hasn't taken us long to recalibrate our expectations. Our psyche of consumption has changed considerably. What was acceptable a decade ago, no longer is. For younger generations, this has become normal commerce. Future generations will expect even more. Order fulfillment will be measured in hours, not days, and the delivery location will be the one that works best for us. It might be your front porch or you may prefer to pick up the order at a kiosk on your way home from work. Alternatively, you might have it placed in the trunk of your car, all while attending to your busy day at the office. Speed of delivery, high inventory availability, and maximum consumer convenience will be the name of the game. You will expect to buy whatever you want, whenever you want it, delivered to the most convenient location, almost instantly.

Most people don't worry about the operational and technological gymnastics that take place in the background to make this all possible. What happens in those few hours after the order button is pressed and before the item shows up at your door? The highly complex, synchronized movement of machines and workers that is launched within seconds is as fascinating as it is astonishing. Understanding the associated processes, capabilities, costs, and limitations will define the difference between success and failure for a growing number of companies.

This book walks through the myriad of technological options in detail, in plain language, using understandable terms. It is not a deeply technical book containing a sea of scientific jargon. It will be valuable to technologists who are new to the space and are motivated to understand the industry quickly, and also to experienced logistics professionals who are seeking to plug some knowledge gaps. It will also be useful to retailers, wholesalers, and third-party logistics providers who face a multitude of automation choices but don't know which way to turn. Those who are considering investing in the space will benefit by understanding what the future is likely to hold. Finally, it will be educational for day-to-day consumers, those who are simply curious and seek to understand what's happening behind the curtain: the highly choreographed movement of machines that continues to turn this modern-day miracle into daily reality.

The Four Industrial Revolutions

When we look back at recent history and the evolution of the four industrial revolutions, we learn about the progress made in manufacturing process automation, steam power, electric power, and a wide range of other technologies. We are now approaching the tail end of the 4th revolution and arguably entering the start of the 5th. This is a world in which we will see greater synchronization of artificial intelligence (AI), smart technologies, robots, and humans. Warehousing and distribution become critical areas of focus, enabling a new set of consumer experiences across a breadth of shopping and service verticals.

The U.S. Federal Reserve's Production Index, which measures the output of all facilities located in the United States for manufacturing, mining, and electric and gas utilities, has increased by 20 times over the past 100 years. According to Statista, a leading data statistics company based in Germany, global trade has increased by 300 times over that same period. Taken together, it is inescapable that we are producing, importing, and exporting orders of magnitude more products today than we did in prior generations, and all this product needs to reach consumers.

Until recently, relatively modest attention was placed on post-manufacturing activities. The manner in which finished goods were stored, transported, and distributed to consumers was treated as necessary evil, a required cost of doing business. The migration of manufacturing to lower-cost countries, including offshoring to the likes of Mexico and

China, has stretched supply chains and turned warehousing and distribution into a critical element of the end-to-end ecosystem. These days, global supply chains break down if warehouses don't operate efficiently or if transportation routes are impeded in any way. Recent pandemic disruptions have made these requirements impossible to ignore.

According to Statista, there were approximately 160,000 large, commercial warehouses in operation globally in 2022, expected to reach 180,000 by 2025. The vast majority of these continue to rely solely on manual processes and manual labor. With ever-increasing consumer expectations, there is a requirement to increase the efficiency of these warehouses. AI, robotics, and cloud systems are being deployed to satisfy this need. It is no longer reasonable to expect human beings, armed with clipboards and manual pick lists, to walk up and down aisles retrieving items from storage racks, transporting them to consolidation and packing locations, or physically wheeling them to shipping docks for manual sortation and truck loading. Simply put, the majority of warehouses in operation today are not fit to handle rapidly evolving consumer demands and expectations.

The Warehousing and Distribution Revolution

The first known warehouses were used to store yields and crops and to better align supply and demand. Since those early days, the rise in commerce has driven an evolution in the supply chain industry. While warehousing was once the supply chain component that received the least focus, it has since been elevated to its core. For some companies, the efficiency of their warehouse processes has become their primary competitive advantage. According to the U.S. Bureau of Labor and Statistics, the rise of warehouse workers has doubled in the past 10 years and tripled in the past 30. It has been fueled by a combined growth of global trade and e-commerce. The turnover in jobs has been notoriously high due to low pay, low job satisfaction, and high numbers of work-related injuries. Attracting people to work in warehouses has become difficult. Maintaining the same labor growth rate as seen in prior decades is unrealistic. The most unpleasant jobs are slowly but surely being replaced by automated alternatives. The good news is that the operation and maintenance needs of the equipment are giving rise to new jobs that offer higher levels of employee satisfaction and better pay.

Warehouses have become increasingly specialized within supply chains. The term warehouse may refer to either a distribution center or a fulfillment center. *Distribution Centers* are essentially merchandise hubs. The products they ship are sent to retail stores, to other distribution centers, or to fulfillment centers. *Fulfillment centers*, on the other hand, primarily support e-commerce or other direct to consumer shipments. Some warehouses do combine distribution and fulfillment activities under one roof.

Warehouse Automation 1.0

In the 1970s and early 1980s, producers (manufacturers) wielded most of the power. Large companies like Procter and Gamble with their multiple brands, addressing a wide variety of consumer needs and with strong marketing, were able to negotiate lucrative deals with retailers. They wielded a position of strength. To purchase the products they wanted, consumers had little option but to drive to their nearest retailer. The retailers, in order to be able to offer those products, were forced to purchase in bulk and to sell off any inventory that wasn't moving, often at large discounts. Manufacturers typically shipped pallet loads of goods to retailers as it was in their best interests to do so. It allowed them to sell more goods and to minimize the overall complexity of their warehouses, effectively "pushing" their products through the supply chain to the consumer. Warehouses were considered cost centers with limited impact on top line revenue. As a result, relatively low levels of investment were being made in them.

Warehouse Automation 2.0

From the mid-1980s through the early 2000s, the power shifted toward retailers. Companies like Walmart grew in strength and they began to wield considerable power over their suppliers. If a manufacturer wanted Walmart to carry their products, they would have to operate by Walmart's rules and agree to their discounts. Manufacturers' warehouses had to change to fit the model. They could no longer force pallet loads of goods on retailers. They often had to break up their pallets and manage the distribution of individual cases as the retailer had much more control over the amount of product they were willing to accept on any given day. Supply chains were forced to become leaner and more responsive and manufacturers had to handle many of the product variability complexities that were previously handled at the retail level.

Warehouse Automation 3.0

By 2010, Amazon's annual revenues grew to over $30B. The bulk of this revenue was generated through e-commerce, of which approximately $12B was in the United States. Statista reported total retail sales in the United States of over $2T in that year, with e-commerce sales accounting for about $170B, or 4.5 percent. At that time, e-commerce sales hit an inflection point, and power began to shift more toward consumers. For the first time, consumers felt less restricted by physical proximity to their favorite stores. Instead, they voted with their wallets, placing a premium on price, product availability, and rapid delivery, forcing retailers to adapt.

Fast forward to 2022. Statista reported total retail sales in the United States of $7.2T, with over 15 percent of it attributed to e-commerce. Analysts estimate that the e-commerce share of the global retail market is even greater, exceeding 20 percent in 2022.

Amazon's sales grew the fastest, surpassing $500B globally in 2022, with over $350B in the United States. Consumers were making new decisions on what they would consume, how much they needed, and where they were going to buy it. Warehouses needed to rethink their operations once again, continuing to fulfill orders from retail outlets in pallets and cases, but also fulfilling them directly to consumers as individual items. Amazon had to figure out how to get that espresso machine to our friend's house in a day or less, which meant dispatching robots into action the moment he clicked the order button. Consumer convenience became paramount and non-Amazon warehouses across the world struggled to compete using processes, systems, and equipment that were quickly becoming obsolete. Retailers found themselves thrust into an omnichannel world with a requirement to fulfill orders through a multitude of channels while adhering to challenging time constraints. Warehouses designed to optimize the storage and movement of goods during the Warehouse Automaton 1.0 and 2.0 eras proved inadequate to satisfy the new agility and flexibility requirements. Investing in automation was required for retailers to keep pace. Warehouse automation companies like Kiva, Swisslog, Dematic, Intelligrated, and Vanderlande became hot commodities and were scooped up by the likes of Amazon, Kuka, KION, Honeywell, and Toyota.

With an annual warehouse automation growth rate already at double-digit levels, COVID served to push that number further into the teens, pouring fuel onto an already well-lit fire. Automate or terminate became the new reality facing many retailers. They witnessed their in-store revenues plummet, snatched up by competitors better positioned to serve consumers' rapidly changing expectations. No retailer benefited from this shift more than Amazon. Many iconic businesses that were unable to react to the changing times began to struggle, and some like Toys R Us, K-Mart, and Sears either liquidated the lion's share of their stores or shut down altogether.

Warehouse Automation 4.0

While we don't yet know exactly how warehouse automation will evolve as we proceed through the second half of the 2020s, we do know it will have a lot to do with advanced robotics, dark-stores, 24×7 operations, networked warehouses, AI, big data, and the ability to better predict the demand for specific goods at specific locations. Realistically, the only way to get goods to consumers faster is to store them closer to the point of demand. With consumers concentrated in urban areas, there is a need to make more efficient use of smaller spaces in those areas. The winners will be those who are able to combine the latest technologies into standardized, small-footprint modules that can be deployed quickly and inexpensively. We explore the various options in this book.

Summarizing the Four Automation Phases

While warehousing activities date back to ancient times, warehouse automation has seen a revolution over the past few decades. Still, the most
significant transformations are likely to be the ones that are still in front
of us. The timelines and characteristics of the four stages of this revolution
are summarized in Table I.1.

*Table I.1 Key characteristics and timeframes of the four warehouse
automation phases*

	Warehouse Automation 1.0	Warehouse Automation 2.0	Warehouse Automation 3.0	Warehouse Automation 4.0
Timeframe	1980s	1990s to early 2000s	Mid-2000s to 2010s	2020s
Power broker	Manufacturer	Retailer	Consumer	Consumer
Automation focus	Pallets	Cases	e-commerce (eaches)	Small urban warehouses (Microfulfillment)
Storage technology	Pallet Cranes	Mini Load cranes	Shuttle systems	Mobile robots
Automation software	Warehouse management system	Warehouse control system	Warehouse execution system	Warehouse Execution system with AI

CHAPTER 1

Warehouse Automation Through the Years

The first Automated Storage and Retrieval System (ASRS), often considered the heart of modern automated warehouses, was developed by Dematic (Demag, at the time) in Germany in the 1960s. Large, sprawling warehouses were difficult to construct in Europe, given the relative scarcity of land. The introduction of ASRSs changed the game. They enabled the full height of the warehouse to be used for the storage and retrieval of goods. They also helped companies manage the impact of rapidly increasing labor costs.

These early ASRSs and their associated rails were initially secured upside down, with racks and masts hanging from the ceiling to help reduce sway. The first production system, which was installed at the Bertelsmann Publishing House in Gütersloh, Germany, is shown in Figure 1.1. It was 20 meters high and had the capacity to store up to 7 million books. It was a pioneering achievement at the time, and it took full advantage of the massive technological investment being made across Europe, most notably in Germany. It set the stage for a new era in warehouse automation.

Warehouse storage was previously stuck at ground level with heavy, palletized goods moved by forklift trucks and conveyors. At times, low-level racking was used to store and retrieve lighter products accessible with Reach Trucks, but heavier products were always stored on the ground. As technological advancements progressed, heavy goods moved upwards and racking, rails and masts were resecured to the ground.

J.C. Penny introduced the Warehouse Management System (WMS) as a game-changing technology in 1975, the first retailer to update stock inventory in real time. Daifuku, a leading provider of automated material handling solutions since the 1960s, deployed its first ASRS at Fujimura

Figure 1.1 The first automated high-bay warehouse installed by Demag at the Bertelsmann publishing house in Wetter, Germany in 1962

Iron Works in Japan in 1972. Despite the relative abundance of warehousing space available in rural areas of North America, by the 1980s, ASRSs began to infiltrate that region as well. Today, 1,000 kg pallet loads can be retrieved by a single crane at rates of approximately 1 pallet per minute, from storage locations as high as 45 meters in the air.

According to Fact.mr, the global ASRS market is not showing any signs of slowing down and is expected to reach $24 billion by 2032, up from approximately $10 billion in 2022. This contributes to the broader warehouse automation market, estimated by Industry Research to be at

$19 billion in 2022, with a Compound Annual Growth Rate (CAGR) of 13.7 percent through 2028. Soaring land and labor costs are driving much of the investment. As in Europe, companies in North America are prioritizing height over footprint when building new warehouses. While Asia Pacific has lagged both Europe and North America in terms of monetary spend in the past, its anticipated CAGR is the highest in the world today. Despite access to relatively low-cost labor, government-led investment in industrialization, the region's population density, and its early embrace of e-commerce have fueled its growth in recent years. Large global warehouse automation providers have also recognized the breadth of opportunities in Asia. Many have elected to open regional headquarters there, declaring it to be one of their strategic growth engines. According to Research Nestor, the size of the warehouse automation market in Asia is expected to reach European and North American levels by 2030. Additionally, there has been a significant increase in the number of Asian companies serving that market, making it difficult for global players to compete effectively on price. Larger Asian manufacturers have also recognized the importance of entering the North American and European markets and are pursuing global growth initiatives of their own.

Warehouse Automation 1.0 Technologies

The 1980s focused on the automation of pallet movement, which was at the core of most manufacturers' operations. Pallets had to be retrieved from storage, conveyed to consolidation areas, and optionally reconfigured before being dispatched to shipping docks via pallet conveyors. The planning cycles that were built into the associated WMS systems were typically measured in days or weeks, rather than hours or minutes. Plans were committed as soon as they were determined, without revalidating them prior to execution.

In some cases, pallets received by warehouses only needed to be cross-docked. These pallets were processed by coordinating the timing of inbound product receipts with outbound shipments, enabling them to be moved directly from one dock door to another. Walmart was the first to popularize automated cross-docking. They had the ability to track the movement of goods throughout their distribution centers and retail stores.

An ASRS that handles pallets, known as a Unit Load system, includes one or more aisles of dual-sided racking, each containing multiple levels. To further increase storage density, double-deep racking may be installed, enabling two pallets to be stored on each side of the aisle. Unit Load cranes move fast, reach the highest levels of tall facilities, and deliver high throughput. The alternative to an ASRS is a fleet of manually operated forklift trucks, which remain popular to this day. Forklift trucks are more restricted in their maximum reach and speed, require more labor, and yield significantly lower throughput rates. They do offer greater flexibility, however, making them the preferred choice for lower throughput, high inventory operations. While the cost of a single high-reach fork truck is considerably less than a crane, the throughput rates, storage density, and labor cost savings associated with an ASRS can result in a return on investment (ROI) in three years or less.

Pallet conveyors, which are used to transport pallets at ground level, are composed of both straight and specialized segments such as inclines, declines, and right-angle transfers (RATs). RATs enable pallets to divert and weave their way around a warehouse.

WMSs control the operation of most modern warehouses. They manage orders and maintain inventory locations and counts in real time. Programmable Logic Controllers (PLCs) and the software that runs on them manage the detailed movement of the machines themselves. Dedicated control software executes the directives received from higher-level software systems (e.g., a WMS). During the Warehouse Automation 1.0 timeframe, there was no strong requirement for sophisticated automation control software, as the primary role of machines was to manage the bulk movement of heavy pallets.

While these warehouses were not overly complicated by today's standards, they did occupy significant square footage. They were erected primarily in rural locations and serviced large regional areas, receiving pallet loads of product from manufacturers and shipping them to retail stores.

Warehouse Automation 2.0 Technologies

As the world entered the Warehouse Automation 2.0 era of the 1990s and 2000s, cases, rather than pallets, became the dominant package size shipped by most warehouses. This change had a significant impact on the operation and complexity of warehouses, including those that invested heavily in pallet-based automation. WMSs became more sophisticated as well, as it became typical for planning cycles to be measured in hours rather than days. Warehouse Control Systems (WCS), the precursor to Warehouse Executions Systems (WES), managed the movement of goods through automation equipment, helping to further increase throughput and reduce cost. Real-time events would trigger replanning cycles to reoptimize prior plans as new data became available.

It was no longer sufficient to store and retrieve palletized products in racks as high as the eye could see. It became increasingly important to store individual cases packed to the ceiling as well, retrieving them when needed, and consolidating them into orders before loading them onto trucks. Unit Load ASRSs didn't disappear as they were still needed for bulk storage of inventory but pallets often had to be broken down into individual cases and re-stored before orders could be processed. A new kind of ASRS dedicated to case handling, Mini Load machines, was created for this purpose. They work much like Unit Load ASRSs, but they move faster, their load capacities are less, and their load-handling devices are telescopic arms, rather than forks.

Two-stage logistics systems comprising a Unit Load ASRS for pallet storage and conveyors for transport evolved into more complicated multistage systems. Unit Load ASRSs and pallet conveyors were still used for bulk storage, retrieval, and transport. In addition, depalletizing stations were used to break pallets into individual cases, Mini Load ASRSs stored and retrieved the cases, case conveyors transported them in and out of the Mini Load system, and high-speed linear sorters, equipped with barcode readers, routed them to their designated shipping areas. Retailers' ability to pressure manufacturers to ship smaller caseloads of product to their stores, impacted the structure of warehouses. The new multistage operations and processes forced many manufacturers to establish partnerships with distributors, leading to the creation of hub-and-spoke networks. Many manufacturers and importers elected to bulk-ship pallet loads of product to their distributors so they could process incoming orders on their behalf. Sophisticated software systems, including WMSs, became vital to manage batch inventory movements in and out of the facility.

Warehouse Automation 3.0 Technologies

As e-commerce grew, the demands facing warehouse operators elevated to new heights. The Warehouse Automation 3.0 era of the 2010s spawned the arrival of many new technologies designed to address the increasingly complex requirements. These technologies extended the ones already in place for pallet and case automation requirements. Now, manufacturers and distributors need to automate the fulfillment of individual items, or "eaches," ordered by an increasing number of consumers through the Internet. Cases had to be broken down so that individual items were ready and waiting to fulfill this new stream of inbound consumer orders. Demands on software systems correspondingly grew. Sophisticated optimization algorithms had to be added to WCSs which gave rise to WESs, enabling planning cycles to be reduced from hours to seconds, and in some cases, subseconds. The practices of "plan and print" that were associated with the warehouse automation 1.0 timeframe, or "plan and replan," associated with the 2.0 timeframe, were changed to "continuous planning" to enable ongoing optimization.

Retailers and distributors who invested in e-commerce-driven automation were facing a choice between two primary alternatives:

- Person-to-Goods (PTG) Picking: Decant individual items into accessible containers for storage on static shelving units, using lights or voice commands to direct the movement of human pickers assigned to different picking zones.
- Goods-to-Person (GTP) Picking: Decant cases into totes stored in ASRS machines such as shuttle systems which retrieve the totes in a required sequence and send them to workstations where associates pick the items and deposit them into order totes.

By automating the storage and retrieval process of totes, they can be delivered rapidly to ergonomic workstations. Workers simply follow the instructions displayed on a computer screen, picking items from donor totes and placing them into adjacent order totes. When an order is complete, the associated tote is dispatched on a conveyor belt to the packing area while the donor totes are returned to storage. A similar process, executed in reverse, is used to replenish goods in the storage system. Improved performance and lower error rates are possible as unproductive walk time is eliminated.

Pallet, Case, and Eaches Picking in the Same Warehouse

For many warehouses, it became necessary to automate a wider array of order processing systems. Pallets needed to be stored, retrieved, or cross-docked to support the requirements of bulk-order customers; cases needed to be stored to support the requirements of a growing number of retail customers; and individual items needed to be stored to support the requirements of e-commerce customers. Inventory availability and rapid delivery expectations increased across all customer segments. Warehouse managers needed to determine how many pallets to break into cases and how many cases to break into eaches. Systems connected Unit Load ASRSs to pallet conveyors, depalletizing machines, case singulators, inbound case conveyors, tote handling ASRS machines, outbound case conveyors, pick workstations, packing stations, labeling and manifest stations, high-speed sorters, and so on. The permutations and combinations, and the number of possible material flow paths, grew exponentially. Each item in the warehouse needed to be tracked with sophisticated software, and processes had to be designed to recover from a variety of failure conditions and unforeseen events.

Warehouse Automation 4.0 Technologies (and Beyond)

Autonomous mobile robots (AMRs), which often use Light Detection and Ranging (LiDAR) technology to gain spatial awareness of their surroundings, are gaining popularity. Enabled with adaptive AI, they can navigate from one location to another without following a predetermined path and can avoid dynamic obstacles (e.g., people, other AMRs) in order to reach their destination. They are manufactured in various shapes and sizes and can support a variety of attachments, each designed to perform a unique task. For example, some AMRs are lighter weight and may be equipped with tilt trays to sort smaller packages. Others have larger weight capacities and are dedicated to pallet transportation. They may move shelving units around to enable GTP picking or may be dispatched to assist pickers in a PTG operation. Regardless of the size or function of an AMR, the units operate as a swarm, controlled by the WES or an associated orchestration engine. The engine dispatches software commands to individual AMRs over the air, instructing them to perform specific tasks. When an AMR completes a task or encounters difficulties, it communicates back and awaits its next command.

Robotic picking is also becoming increasingly popular. Articulated arm robots with integrated grippers, 2D and 3D cameras, and machine-learning software, will eventually replace human pickers. They are able to robotically pick items from donor totes and place them into order totes or onto conveyors. The speed, accuracy, and cost of these robots make them difficult to cost-justify in some environments but improvements are happening rapidly. The level of investment in robotic picking technologies is expected to increase significantly over the next several years.

As we proceed through the early part of the 2020s, e-commerce is expected to drive a transition toward micro-fulfillment. Micro-fulfillment centers (MFCs), sometimes located in the back of large box stores, are configured with standardized automation equipment, enabling orders to be fulfilled in a location that's just around the corner from the consumer. The MFC model offers a number of advantages (e.g., rapid delivery, simplified returns, and flexible pickup options) but also introduces several challenges. Ensuring inventory availability in the right quantity and location requires sophisticated demand planning software. It also requires a new level of software functionality that looks beyond the four walls of the warehouse, enabling multiple MFCs to operate in a network as a virtual fulfillment center. Orders may be fulfilled from multiple MFCs and each MFC may replenish depleted inventory levels of neighboring ones. Inventory must be updated in real-time with network-level visibility. Additionally, orders should be able to reserve inventory in any networked warehouse. These micro-warehouses, which are changing the very definition of a warehouse, require increased levels of reliability due to the lack of knowledgeable, permanent service personnel. Despite the challenges, micro-fulfillment is expected to increase in adoption as we proceed through the decade and as new technology companies enter the fold. The grocery industry is leading the way but other verticals are watching closely and are expected to follow suit as the technology matures.

Key Takeaways

- Warehouse Automation first gained attention in the early 1980s when Unit Load ASRSs, pallet conveyors, and WMSs were used more widely to automate the transport of heavy pallets.
- In the 1990s and 2000s, warehouse automation expanded to support case loads as retailers were less likely to accept full pallets of goods from manufacturers. Automated equipment and software increased in complexity as a result.
- In the early 2010s, e-commerce gained traction and end-consumers began to wield more power. Vendors were forced to offer retailers more sophisticated, automated each-picking solutions.
- In the 2020s, more flexible automated warehouses using AMRs, robotic picking, and AI-based software became popular. A shift toward smaller warehouses in urban areas began to surface in parallel. These trends are expected to continue through the balance of the decade and likely beyond.

CHAPTER 2

The Case for Automation

Automation broadly impacts a company's performance on both sides of the profit and loss equation. It lowers costs and alters the balance between operational and capital expenditures. The effect of automation on the revenue side has moved to the foreground with the emergence of e-commerce and its need to maintain service level agreements (SLAs) that manual processes cannot guarantee.

Cost Considerations

Labor Costs

The traditional justification for investing in automation is cost reduction, especially direct costs related to labor per shipment or unit of fulfillment throughput. To achieve operational cost efficiency, automation investments include fixed and indirect expenditures associated with capital, equipment depreciation, and the operation of the system itself. The latter includes energy, consumables, maintenance, and repairs. Automation also incurs indirect labor costs to maintain the equipment, usually requiring higher qualifications and pay levels than the direct labor used in manual operations.

Unlike manufacturing, warehousing and distribution is an industry that requires a local presence. This largely prevents the use of off-shoring to reduce labor costs and forces the logistics industry to compete with other employers for lower-skill labor. According to the U.S. Bureau of Labor and Statistics, employment in the U.S. warehousing and storage industry has almost tripled over the past 10 years. During the same period, the hourly cost of labor has risen by about 25 percent.

Europe is witnessing similar trends, with the added challenges of reduced population growth putting even more pressure on the cost of labor. Europe's strong unions introduce an additional level of uncertainty on labor availability due to frequent contract negotiations and associated strikes. Even in developing economies, rising education levels and the globalization of manufacturing and services are forcing logistics operators to compete against higher-paying jobs. From a cost perspective, the replacement of direct labor with indirect labor is normally advantageous. The evolution of automation systems, with increased reliability and connectivity to cloud-based Internet of Things (IoT) monitoring and management systems, is reducing the cost of automation operations, making the investment easier to justify.

Real Estate Costs

Availability of land and space for logistics operations has followed the general trends of real estate markets, driven by population density, expanding metropolitan areas, and a general scarcity of land near economic activity centers. As reported by Cushman & Wakefield, the cost of property rentals in the United States has doubled in the last 10 years.

In the past, warehousing and logistics operators were able to contain real estate costs of large regional distribution centers by moving them to less populated areas where land was cheap and relatively available. This solution is now less feasible. Metropolitan areas are expanding, and logistics hubs are beginning to feel the pressure of urbanization. More importantly, the expectation of shorter e-commerce delivery times is forcing fulfillment centers to open closer to the demand. Space for warehouses is at a premium, forcing them to operate with higher densities.

Evaluating the Level of Investment

In order to optimize the level of automation spend, an organization must analyze six primary parameters:

- Expected shipment volume or throughput of the facility
- Baseline costs per unit (of the existing manual operation)
- Investment cost per unit of throughput
- Direct cost per unit (of the automated operation)

- Maximum throughput growth expected during the life of the investment
- Availability of capital and the risk tolerance of the organization

On a first approximation, the optimal level of investment provides the lowest total cost per unit at nominal throughput, with the maximum capacity capable of handling the projected throughput over the life of the investment.

Figure 2.1 shows three idealized investment scenarios comparing different automation levels. Low automation, which relies significantly on labor; high automation, where most operations are automated; and mid-automation, which includes a combination of both. The low-automation scenario works well at lower volumes but has a relatively high baseline cost per unit of throughput. High automation, with its high fixed costs, is not competitive at low volumes. Mid-automation becomes increasingly competitive in the lower volume range as it begins to increase. Mid- and high-level automation systems tend to have hard

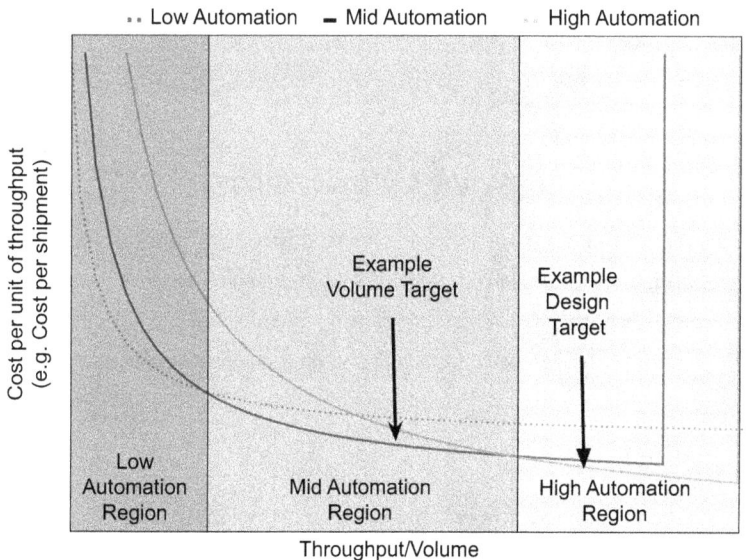

Figure 2.1 The target throughput and the range at which automation offers cost advantages in comparison to a manual operation

limits on throughput as a byproduct of their design, depicted in the figure as vertical lines at their maximum throughput levels.

Underinvestment in automation will result in higher costs per unit of throughput and an increased likelihood of encountering capacity constraints. This impacts potential revenue growth and forces an organization to find alternative fulfillment capacity, typically at a higher cost. On the other hand, overinvestment may result in higher costs per unit of throughput due to underutilized capacity. As shown in Figure 2.1, attempting to balance these considerations may lead to choosing a design point (right arrow) that exceeds the stated volume requirements (left arrow) if future growth is anticipated. The chosen design point needs to balance dimensioning for peak growth, capital constraints, and the risks associated with growth forecasts.

When evaluating the cost per unit, the volumetric utilization of a physical facility must also be considered. Automation improves storage density and throughput of a given facility. It enables higher storage positions to be productively used, which is critical when real estate is expensive. E-commerce is driving the creation of MFCs to store inventory as close to the consumer as possible, driving up real estate costs in urban areas and making automation even more important. When estimating space requirements, it is important to account for maintenance areas and passages, as well as space for ancillary equipment and control rooms.

Revenue Considerations

The revenue impact of automation can be difficult to quantify and measure, and it is often underestimated. Over the past 10 years, with the rise of e-commerce, the impact of automation on revenue has grown and it now must be considered when evaluating an automation project.

The Tyranny of Now

E-Commerce has led toward customer expectations of instant fulfillment ("the tyranny of now") and endless product variations and options ("The infinite shelf").

In the last 10 years, in addition to the scarcity of labor and space, consumer behaviors have pushed the industry well beyond its traditional capabilities to handle the required volumes and order variability and expanded the boundary of automation's technological capabilities.

Consumers expect to buy whatever they want and have it delivered to their doorsteps within a day or less, or they will look elsewhere. Retailer loyalty has all but disappeared. Traditional performance metrics (e.g., cost per unit shipped, units shipped per period) have taken a back seat to customer-centric metrics (e.g., time to fulfill, order accuracy). If one combines these expectations with the scarcity of labor and space, the result is an intense pressure driving an ever-increasing demand for innovation.

Fulfillment Excellence Through Automation

Revenue in fulfillment and distribution operations is determined by the ability to fulfill a high volume of orders accurately and on time. The impact on revenue measured by the number of orders that can be fulfilled by a facility is self-evident, with automation enabling higher throughput levels. Its reduced reliance on labor and its ability to extend operating hours improves the effective capacity of a facility. Failure to ship accurately or on time results in a loss of both short and long-term revenue, due to the impact on customer satisfaction and brand reputation.

Automated systems have more accurate and up-to-date inventory information than manual systems. Accurate inventory records eliminate order fulfillment exceptions when inventory is overestimated. Additionally, the fulfillment of orders cannot be committed when inventory availability is underestimated.

Improved inventory accuracy also enables distribution and fulfillment centers to reduce the amount of safety stock needed to operate. Reduced safety stock levels can render savings similar to those realized by increased storage densities. The space freed up by carrying less stock per stock keeping unit (SKU) can be used to carry a broader range of goods.

Automated operations display a much lower variation in order fulfillment times than manual operations, with fewer exceptions and more consistent pick/pack/ship processes. Delays in order fulfillment lead to potential order cancellation issues and loss of future revenue due to customer attrition.

Understanding the Technology Investment

Operations/Technologies Map

To understand the impact of technology, it is useful to characterize the range of operations that take place in warehouses. Logistics operations tend to be more flexible and less specialized than those in manufacturing. Figure 2.2 depicts logistics operations through the two classical dimensions of volume and variability.

In the bottom right quadrant, we have low volume, high variability operations that rely heavily on manual operations, usually managed with a traditional WMS with little if any automation. Typical examples are small retail/e-commerce fulfillment centers, small Third-Party Logistics (3PL) distributors, and specialty goods operators like spare parts distributors. In the top left quadrant, we have high-volume "flow" operations

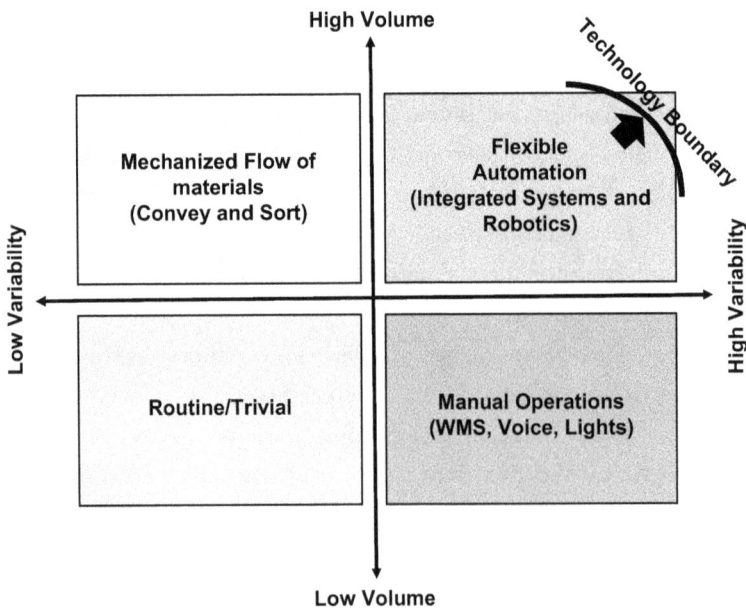

Figure 2.2 A depiction of the types of technology deployed in varying warehouse environments

with limited variability. An example of this is parcel and mail distribution. In these environments, parcels are all handled largely the same way and the volume is very high. Retail distribution, with its fairly large volumes, limited variability, and frequently repeated "replenishment" orders, is another example of automation in this quadrant. The traditional middle ground, shown skewed to the upper right of center, is associated with mid-market, high SKU-count retail operations that have benefited from advancements in flexible automation technologies. On one side of this "state of the art" line, there are trivial operations, with low volume and low variability that can be managed using ad-hoc processes and tools (e.g., paper and clipboard). In the top right quadrant, we find the performance boundary defined by the current level of technology. By nature, this boundary is dynamic and changes as increased levels of investment are made in the technologies that serve the industry.

Impact of Emerging Technologies

Fortunately, evolving trends in emerging technologies provide tools to help relieve the pressure.

1. Computation power and communication bandwidth are becoming ubiquitous and inexpensive, with continuously decreasing costs. This enables programmable logic to be embedded in operations that would not have been able to support the cost in the past.
2. Software platforms and programming models have greatly improved the productivity of application developers and their ability to tackle more complex problems (e.g., cloud computing platforms, micro-services, etc.).
3. Machine learning (ML) and artificial intelligence (AI) have matured to the point that useful facts and decisions can be drawn by processing and classifying large amounts of semistructured and unstructured data.

These trends have enabled a new generation of automation systems that support more modular, flexible, and less capital-intensive solutions. For example, inexpensive computation has led to distributed control systems and sensor-rich automation systems. Cloud computing and the development practices that evolved with it have lowered the cost of deployments and the operation and maintenance of these systems. Finally, ML is producing better planning results and shorter exception-handling times than traditional optimization algorithms.

Applying Automation Effectively

Different warehouse processes respond differently to automation investments and have varying impacts on cost and revenue. As a general rule, processes that focus on Receiving to Storage should optimize for cost reduction, while processes that focus on Storage through Shipping should target improvements in capacity and throughput.

Inbound Processes

Cost reduction associated with inbound process automation is accomplished by improving the accuracy of the inventory and the optimization of dock utilization. In distribution warehouses, inbound processing tends to occur in batches with idle periods between them. Although there are dedicated solutions for unloading and receiving, it often makes sense to deploy equipment that can be repurposed for other tasks during these idle times, such as Automated Guided Vehicles (AGVs) and AMRs. While the efficiency gains may be lower, the cost of these solutions can be amortized across other processes in the warehouse. To improve accuracy, dedicated identification systems like barcode scanners and Radio Frequency Identification (RFID) systems are often used. The investments lead to increased inventory accuracy, improved fulfillment capabilities, early detection of defects, and faster allocation of inventory to orders.

Dock availability can be a bottleneck in inbound operations. In low-volume operations, docks are scheduled manually or on a first-come-first-served basis. For higher volume facilities, this may not be feasible. Appointment systems to schedule the docks and to dispatch workers and equipment to the receiving area are essential to maintain the flow of materials through the warehouse.

Storage

Storage automation, especially for bulk storage, is justified by the spatial density improvements in comparison to manual operations. Higher spatial density is achieved through the use of higher storage levels, narrower aisle widths, and in highly constrained environments, storage of pallets at multiple depths using special manipulators. The increased density leads to a reduction in the size and cost of the facility and frees up space for revenue-generating activities. For forward-pick locations, the investment leads to reduced inventory fetch time variability which helps make ship times more predictable.

Order Fulfillment Activities

Automation has the highest investment return in core fulfillment processes as it impacts all the cost and revenue elements mentioned above. Picking, Packing, Order Preparation, and Outbound activities are the most labor intensive in a distribution warehouse. Automation directly addresses those labor costs. It also maximizes the throughput of a given facility. As an example, GTP stations can increase pick rates up to 1,000 picks per hour, with the additional potential of increasing the hours of operation. Automation in fulfillment also reduces inventory count errors, incorrect shipments, and offers faster and more predictable order-to-ship lead times. The combination of these factors results in increased customer satisfaction and revenues, or at a minimum, reduced customer attrition. An often-overlooked benefit of automation in the fulfillment area is improved traceability of shipments to customer orders. This is accomplished through inspection, labeling, scanning, and data tracking (e.g., lot or serial numbers), all contributing to lower costs of product recalls, consumer returns, and disputes.

A New World

Order ship time improvements and adherence to on-time commitments have become a right-of-entry capability in the e-commerce space. Without operational and technology changes, fulfillment operations cannot meet the required performance standards and companies will lose revenue to competitors who are more able to meet expectations. Manual operations, without the aid of at least some level of automation technology, are too unpredictable to achieve the required performance targets with any level of consistency.

Improvements in automation technology (e.g., robotic picking, autonomous vehicles, vision systems, etc.) have created opportunities in areas that were not previously considered to be candidates for automation, such as picking, case palletizing, quality control, and inventory counting. When a complete end-to-end process can be automated, such as mixed-case palletizing in grocery fulfillment, it can create a domino effect on adjacent processes. The uncertainty of labor availability is no longer just a matter of cost but it has become a business resilience liability. The lack of people to perform these jobs is actually threatening growth plans and constraining companies in developing customers and markets. Automation is no longer just a cost reduction tool but an indispensable foundation for the execution of companies' plans. Even when there is sufficient access to labor, it is more uncertain than it has been in the past. The need to hedge against these disruptions has further driven the development and adoption of automation technologies. In the last few years, external factors like weather (e.g., hurricanes, fires) and the pandemic have made access to labor even more uncertain. Automation now plays a role in business continuity plans and enables more distributed and remote organizations to keep operating in the face of these disruptions.

Key Takeaways

- In modern distribution and fulfillment operations, warehouse automation has an impact on both cost and revenue and both need to be considered when evaluating automation investments.
- Revenue impact, although harder to quantify, affects the strategy and competitive positioning of a company.
- The level of investment needs to take into account not only the target operational scale but also the expectations of growth and estimation uncertainties.

- The types of technologies to apply depend on the throughput and variability characteristics of the associated operations.
- While all areas of the warehouse are candidates for automation, outbound processes often have the highest impact as they affect revenue and customer service directly.

CHAPTER 3

The Big Picture—Receiving to Shipping

When we analyze the various functions performed in a warehouse, it doesn't take long to see that they include a complicated sequence of highly choreographed processes with a multitude of feedback loops. Automating a warehouse efficiently is a daunting task, made somewhat less daunting when done in stages.

A Bird's Eye View

This book focuses on activities that take place within the four walls of a warehouse which is just one element of the overall supply chain. What happens outside of those four walls does, however, impact the actions that need to be taken within them. A supplier's ability to deliver orders as scheduled and a carrier's ability to arrive on time to pick up outbound shipments are direct inputs to the operational systems of a warehouse. Warehouses must continually manage exceptions and update task plans by maintaining visibility into the movement of products and operational events outside of their four walls. All core supply chain systems must communicate in real time to operate efficiently. Delayed arrivals must be anticipated so the WMS can decide whether to postpone a complete shipment or to short-ship a partial one. Software is the orchestration engine that binds the various supply chain processes together. Figure 3.1 depicts the core elements of supply chain management systems at a high level. The shaded portion highlights the primary areas of focus of this book. The software components are described in detail in Chapter 12. WMS software is deployed in both manual and automated warehouses, focusing on features like inventory management and order management. WCS and WES software are deployed only in automated environments,

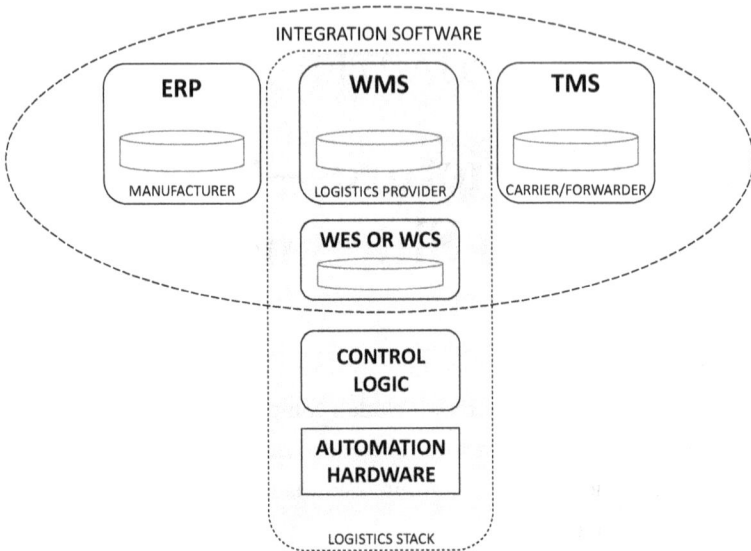

Figure 3.1 The software components that are most relevant to supply chain management are depicted in the diagram. Manufacturers rely most heavily on Enterprise Resource Planning Application (ERP) systems. Logistics providers and wholesalers rely on a broad logistics stack including a WMS, a WCS or WES, and specialized control software to manage the physical movement of the automation equipment. Carriers and forwarders rely primarily on Transportation Management Systems (TMS) to manage their businesses

with a focus on the efficient movement of goods through a connected series of automated machines and human interactions.

Figure 3.2 highlights the main operational processes that exist in a warehouse. Any subset of these may be automated. Specific facilities will prioritize different processes as their primary targets for automation. What to automate and the details behind the automation are heavily influenced by the industry being served and by the role of the warehouse in the supply chain. Some industries focus exclusively on bulk, pallet-level shipments of heavier items to retailers. Some focus on the storage and distribution of perishable products, managing multiple temperature zones, and a need to comply with strict regulations, timing, and chain of custody constraints. Others deal exclusively with direct-to-consumer, smaller-quantity e-commerce orders where rapid delivery is paramount. For these orders, fulfillment cycle time is critically important. Machines

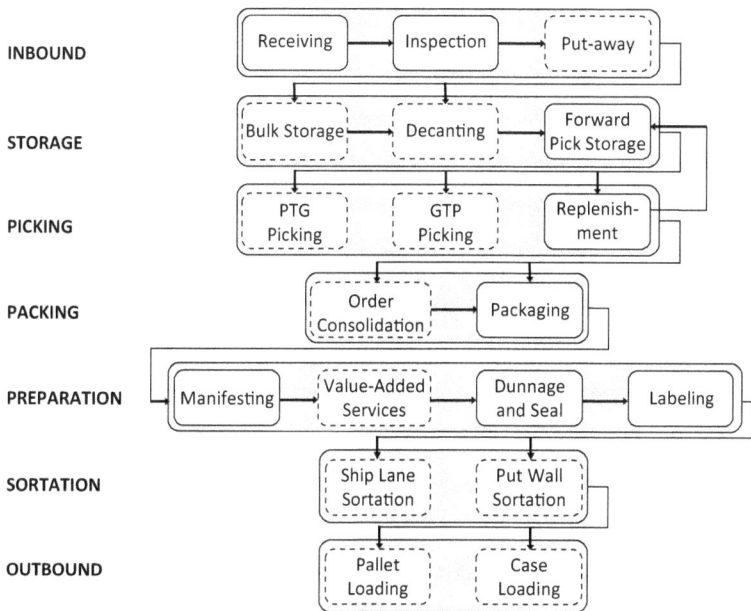

Figure 3.2 *The main processes involved in managing a warehouse are depicted. Optional processes are shown with dashed lines. Warehouse operators may choose to automate any subset of these processes. In the most sophisticated warehouses, almost all processes are automated*

must begin to move soon after an order button is clicked on a mobile device or home computer. We walk through the various processes at a high level in this chapter, without getting buried in details, and without considering the various alternatives or exceptions. We dive into more detail in subsequent chapters.

Inbound

Trucks carrying goods arrive at inbound loading docks throughout the day. To operate efficiently, Advanced Shipping Notices (ASNs) are electronically sent ahead of time by shipping companies to the WMS. The ASN informs the warehouse of the products to expect, the physical characteristics of each product, when the shipment is scheduled to arrive, and the mode of transportation being used. Warehouse operators can plan for the arrival of shipments by preassigning dock doors and personnel to unload the goods.

Receiving

Once a truck arrives at the dock, the receiving process begins. Docks are one of the scarcest resources in a warehouse as they are shared between shipping and receiving processes and can be a bottleneck in achieving targeted throughput levels.

Manual receiving processes utilize forklift trucks to remove the pallets from trailers and deposit them in staging areas. Alternatively, a number of fully automated options are available, usually for pallet retrieval. Dedicated solutions for automating the retrieval of pallets in slugs are one option and more general-purpose AGV offerings provide another.

Inspection

Once products have been received, they may be inspected before being recorded into inventory. Damaged products are returned to suppliers and the associated attributes may be recorded for later use and analysis. Inspection may be done manually or by using an assortment of automated tools. The earlier that product issues are detected in a warehouse, the lower the downstream remediation costs.

Put-Away

Once products have been inspected, a decision is made whether to move them to designated bulk storage locations or to make them immediately available to fulfill existing or anticipated orders. It may make sense to remove products from their shipping containers on receipt and send them straight to forward-pick locations.

A detailed discussion of automated inbound processing options is the focus of Chapter 4.

Storage

The approach to storage management varies considerably across warehouses. Storage technologies deployed within a specific vertical industry are usually similar but they tend to vary significantly across industries.

Bulk Storage

After products have been inspected, they are ready to be put away to bulk storage. In a manual operation, these locations may be nothing more than areas of allocated floor space or steel racking systems, perhaps in a relatively remote location of the warehouse. In an automated warehouse, inbound products may be moved to an ASRS. Pallets, or cases, will be retrieved from bulk storage at a future point in time as determined by the WES.

An inbound conveyor system, be it a pallet conveyor or a case conveyor, may be used to transport products toward bulk storage. Some warehouses use AGVs or AMRs, which offer increased flexibility and range. The WES determines the physical storage location to use and strives to avoid bottlenecks.

Decanting

Unless the packaging of inbound products matches customer orders, decanting is required. Decanting refers to the unpacking of products so they can be stored and tracked as individual units of inventory. If products at forward-pick locations are in short supply and need of replenishment, inbound items may be sent directly to decanting stations. Otherwise, the WES will monitor the quantity and rate of consumption of each product at each forward pick location. When the quantity drops below a defined threshold, the WES initiates a replenishment process by requesting more products from bulk storage.

Forward Pick Storage

Unlike bulk storage, forward-pick storage is often located in a central area of the warehouse, making it easier for human pickers to access the items. Offering rapid access to stored items, it can be viewed as cache storage, not unlike cache memory in a computer. Figure 3.3 shows a simple graphic of the relationship between bulk storage and forward-pick storage.

In a GTP system, this cache storage often takes the form of a specialized ASRS like a shuttle system, which can rapidly retrieve totes or cases

```
                  ┌─────────────────────────────────────────────┐
                  │                                             │
                  │              Bulk Storage                   │
Receiving  ┄┄┄┄┄─┤                                             │
                  │                                             │
                  └──────────┬──────────────────┬──────────────┘
                             │                  │
                      Replenishment             │
                             │                  │
                  ┌──────────┴─────────┐        │
                  │                    │        │
                  │ Forward Pick Storage│   (Expensive) Order
                  │                    │   Assignment
                  │                    │        │
                  └──────────┬─────────┘        │
                             │                  │
                      Order Assignment          │
```

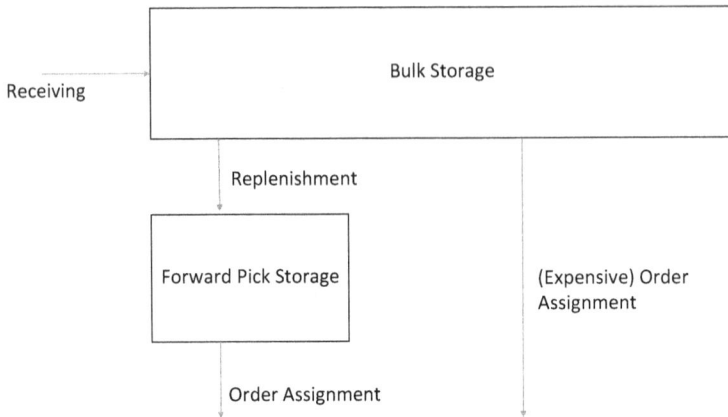

Figure 3.3 Bulk storage is used to store products for longer periods of time, usually on pallets and in the same form as it was received from suppliers. When the products are needed for immediate assignment to orders, they are pulled out from bulk storage, decanted, and stored in forward pick locations

for assignment to orders. It is faster and less expensive to pick an item from a forward pick location than from bulk storage.

Products that are ordered often are referred to as fast movers and those ordered infrequently as slow movers. Allocating low-latency storage to fast-moving products may be important as not all forward-pick locations are the same. Fast movers may be stored in a location that minimizes walk time in a PTG system and wait time in a GTP system.

A detailed discussion of automated storage is presented in Chapter 5.

Picking

Picking takes two forms: Single-Order Picking and Multi-Order Picking. In the former, all items of an order are picked and dropped into an order tote with no requirement for a downstream consolidation phase. In the latter, items crossing multiple orders are picked into one or more totes and a downstream consolidation phase separates them into individual orders. Multi-Order Picking has the advantage of speeding up the picking process but it comes at the expense of a secondary consolidation phase. Single-Order Picking is slower from a pick rate perspective but it doesn't require a secondary step, nor the additional cost of a consolidation station.

PTG Picking

In a PTG environment, goods are stored in forward-pick locations on static racks. All pick locations are clearly marked. Locations are organized into sections and each section is referred to as a zone, with pickers assigned to work in one or more zones. Zones are composed of one or more aisles, usually with racks on both sides. Racks are further subdivided into levels and shelving units, with each unit encompassing multiple, numbered storage locations, or slots. WMS algorithms attempt to optimize slotting for each SKU and to reduce the pick and replenishment times for fast-moving products. Operators are instructed by the system to move to designated locations to pick the required quantity of inventory.

PTG picking can be made more efficient by introducing a variety of technologies. The simplest approach is pure manual picking, where employees are handed preprinted pick sheets, which guide them through a predetermined path. It's not particularly efficient, flexible, or fast, and it can be error prone, but it is inexpensive. Alternatively, each location may be configured with lights. In this case, clipboards are discarded and pickers wait for their assigned light color to illuminate. Radio Frequency (RF) picking is another option. Pickers strap a small handset with a built-in RF gun to their arms. The screen on the handset directs them to the next pick location. Voice picking is also possible. Automated voice directives are sent to pickers through wireless headsets and they acknowledge completed picks via voice confirmations.

Regardless of the method used, picked products are deposited into totes (for "each" picking) or onto pallets or transport modules (for case picking) and moved to a downstream zone for additional picking or consolidation or packing areas.

GTP Picking

GTP solutions are significantly more expensive and complex than their PTG counterparts. The core of a GTP solution is the storage and sequencing system. Cases or totes are stored in optimized locations within the system, retrieved as directed by the WES, and sent to picking stations located at the end of each aisle. The ergonomically designed stations are designed to handle one or more donor and order totes at the same time, with the WES directing workers to pick the designated number of items from each donor tote and deposit them into the specified order totes. When an order tote is full, or when an order is complete, it is moved to the packing area. Donor totes are sent back to storage when all picks from them are complete.

There are a variety of automation technologies used in GTP systems, all of which are discussed in Chapters 5 and 6. Once the items have been retrieved from storage, the actual picking operation takes place at the pick station. Pick stations vary from simple areas where totes are delivered by conveyors, to ergonomically optimized machines where goods are presented to an operator in a manner that minimizes effort, idle time, and unnecessary movement.

Replenishment

Whether using PTG or GTP, goods must be replenished into forward storage locations when available quantities fall below thresholds. The process is the reverse of the picking process. In a GTP environment, totes are retrieved from storage, transported to workstations, and supplemented with additional items that were inducted into the system. In a PTG system, goods are replenished by workers manually, usually at the back of the rack. The WES maintains a count of all products at all locations and determines the best time to initiate a replenishment cycle.

Packing

Once orders have been picked, they are sent downstream to the packing area for order consolidation (if required) and packaging.

Order Consolidation

There are a number of ways that items associated with multiorder picks may be consolidated into individual orders. Two of the most popular are unit sorters and Put Walls.

A unit sorter moves individual transport cells around in a loop, with discharge chutes positioned throughout the perimeter. As an item approaches its designated discharge chute, the WES instructs the cell's mechanism to fire, moving the item off the sorter.

A Put Wall is composed of multiple compartments that resemble mail slots, sometimes of varying sizes. As the totes arrive at a Put Wall, individual items are retrieved and scanned. With each scan, the WES directs the worker to put the item into the designated location. When all items composing an order have arrived, another worker empties the contents of the compartment into a designated container or carton.

Packaging

Once items have been consolidated into orders, they are ready for packaging. Like other warehouse processes, the packaging phase can be performed manually or automated. In the most basic environments, a worker chooses the best package size from a selection of options. In more advanced environments, the WES or WMS selects the most appropriate packaging option to use, calculating it based on a variety of parameters.

Preparation

After items have been assigned to shipping containers, be they envelopes, bags, cases, or pallets, they must be prepared for shipping.

Manifesting

Retailers and distributors usually include a manifest, or packing slip, inside or outside a package to identify its contents. This is particularly important when shipping multi-item orders and when orders are split into multiple boxes. It enables validation before a package is sealed and it helps recipients confirm that all expected items were received. It also informs recipients when some items in an order have been shipped separately. In the case of international shipping, a packing slip or bill of lading (BOL) may be used by customs authorities to assess the value of a shipment.

Value Added Services

Additional services, such as kitting, gift wrapping, quality checking, assembly, or preassembly, may take place within a warehouse. With an increasing focus on sustainability, offering these services directly eliminates the transportation cycle required when they are performed at a different facility.

Value Added Services (VAS) may be integrated directly into the fulfillment process. Some orders require them and others do not. The WES manages the movement of the goods through designated stations and displays the instructions to the associate. The WES also passes the information back to the WMS or ERP to ensure all associated financial transactions are handled.

Dunnage, Seal, and Label

Before a package is sealed for shipping, a decision must be made on the type of protective material (dunnage) to use. Dunnage may take multiple forms. While the physical application of dunnage is usually done manually, the WES must select the material to use and provide corresponding instructions to the worker via a computer monitor. Automated dunnage application options are available as well but are usually implemented when only a single material is used.

Once dunnage has been inserted, a package is ready to be sealed. The way it is performed depends on the unit being shipped. If it is a pallet, it is done with stretch wrap. If the unit is a cardboard case, sealing tape may be applied manually or by using an automated box sealer. Most automated solutions handle a variety of box sizes and are easily integrated with case conveyors.

The final packaging step is labeling. The process is referred to as Label, Print, and Apply (LPA). It involves the selection of an appropriate label format for the package and transportation carrier, the printing of the required information, and the application of the label to the exterior of the package. The process begins by scanning the barcode contained on the package. Most LPA machines have built-in scanners, scales, and dimension checkers to ensure labels are applied at an appropriate location on the packages.

The details associated with automated packing and preparation are described in Chapter 7.

Sortation

After labeling is complete, packages are sent to their designated shipping lanes. In a manual warehouse, pallets are moved using forklift trucks. By scanning the barcode of the pallet, the WMS informs a forklift driver of the designated shipping bay. In an automated warehouse, pallets are transported via pallet conveyors, monorails, or AGVs, winding through a facility and diverting them to their required locations. In manual warehouses, smaller packages may be wheeled in carts to consolidation areas. In automated environments, they are usually transported via conveyors before being inducted onto a shipping lane sorter. The details associated with the various sortation options are described in Chapter 8.

Ship Lane Sortation

Ship lane sortation may be managed using automated sorters, such as Crossbelts, Tilt Trays, Bombay, Sliding Shoe, or Activated Roller Belts (ARB™). Alternatively, AMRs can combine sortation and transportation, inducting items onto a small conveyor segment or a tilt tray attached to the top of the AMR.

When products arrive at their designated shipping lanes, be they pallets or cases, they are staged in preparation for truck loading. The goal is to load the truck in the most efficient sequence and as quickly as possible. The WMS manages the dock door allocations and their associated timing windows.

Put Wall Sortation

If sortation rate requirements are modest, manual or automated Put Walls may be deployed to sort packaged goods, similar to the way they sort items into orders. Shipping labels are scanned to illuminate a light adjacent to a designated compartment. In the case of an automated Put Wall, a case is automatically transported and diverted to a designated bin. Each bin or compartment corresponds to a shipping lane.

Outbound

The last step in processing orders in a warehouse is the outbound process. It is responsible for loading trucks in a delivery-friendly order, either with palletized products or with loose packages. Once the products have been loaded, warehouse inventory counts are updated.

Before a truck arrives at a warehouse door to pick up a load, a set of electronic messages are exchanged between the TMS and the WMS. The WMS is informed of the expected arrival time, the orders to be picked up, the truck loading order (if relevant), and so on. It responds to the TMS with the assigned loading dock number and its associated time window.

Regardless of how a truck is loaded, the WMS must produce a BOL to itemize all products loaded onto the truck, including customer order numbers, the number of packages included with each order, the package weights, handling instructions, shipper details, carrier details, and so on. The BOL represents the official contract between the warehouse and the carrier and it must be signed off by an authorized representative of the carrier.

Pallet Loading

Not surprisingly, the pallet-loading process is the reverse of the pallet-unloading process. When automated, the two processes often use the same technology. Even in a manual warehouse, truck loading software may be used to assist forklift drivers to efficiently load a truck. Some automated systems enable loading to be done in one shot, after preparing slugs in an adjacent staging area. AGVs may also be used to automate the loading process. While they are slower than purpose-built truck-loading systems, they offer much more flexibility.

Loose Loading

Loading of loose cartons onto trucks is one of the most challenging tasks to automate in a warehouse. With relatively limited room to maneuver, and the requirement for precise placements to ensure boxes are stacked in a stable fashion, articulated arm robots offer the most promise. Speed, density, and cost are limiting most production-level implementations, though that is expected to change in the coming years. An alternative is to load cases into custom racks or large containers, which are then loaded onto a truck in one shot. While several of these systems have been designed, few, if any, have been successfully commercialized. Further detail on staging and automated truck loading is covered in Chapter 9.

Key Takeaways

- The core processes of a warehouse are inbound processing, storage, picking, packing, preparation, sortation, and outbound processing.
- Each process includes a number of subprocesses, some mandatory and some optional.
- Warehouses may execute all processes manually, automate a small subset of critical processes or subprocesses, or operate in an almost fully automated manner.
- Most facilities start small and grow their automation investments over time. The number of automated processes usually expand as business and throughput requirements demand it, and as the associated cost becomes justifiable.

CHAPTER 4

Automated Receiving and Inspection

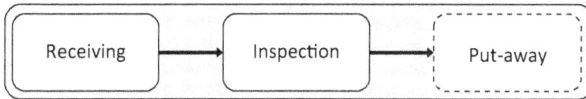

As the old saying goes, "garbage in, garbage out." A warehouse is no different. In the case of its operation, care must be taken to minimize the likelihood that garbage (inaccurate or damaged goods) is inducted into inventory as it can lead to snowballing downstream operational costs. That being said, each business case must be analyzed carefully to ensure that automation expenses are weighed against the expected tangible benefits.

Warehouse operations begin with inbound processing, the receiving of goods into the physical environment, and the recording of the new inventory into the system of record. The following steps are involved:

- Truck-to-dock-door assignment
- Truck manifest verification
- Unloading of physical goods to a staging location
- Physical counting of goods to verify inventory (optional)
- Receipt of goods into the system of record (WMS), usually against a purchase order
- Physical Inspection of goods (optional) and the assignment of a disposition

The form in which goods are received (pallets, cases, eaches, and bulk) determines the associated inbound processes and the automation technologies that may be used.

Truck to Dock Door Assignment

The process of assigning trucks to dock doors sounds simple enough but there's more to it than meets the eye. Imagine a busy warehouse with multiple receiving docks. Trucks arrive and depart all day long. When one arrives or is expected to arrive, a dock door may be assigned to it for a period of time to support the unloading or loading operation. Unexpected issues, like loading or unloading delays of an earlier truck, can make the best-laid plans go awry. Sophisticated logic is required to manage the allocation of dock doors, forecast the times they will be busy with each truck, and react to unexpected delays.

Dock scheduling software is designed to address this need. It is available from several independent vendors as extensions of WMS offerings or as stand-alone cloud-based solutions. Short Message Service (SMS) or Electronic Data Interchange (EDI) communication is frequently used to send information between a carrier and the warehouse. The carrier informs the warehouse of its expected arrival time, its contents, and trailer type. The scheduling software acknowledges the request and assigns a dock door, transmitting the door number and a reservation window to the carrier. The same process is used when an empty truck is enroute to a warehouse to pick up a shipment. Dock sensors may be installed to provide real-time status information on the dock and to alert the scheduling software of any changes.

Yard management software (YMS) works hand-in-hand with dock scheduling software. When a truck arrives at the entrance gate of a warehouse and a dock door is not available, the driver is admitted to the yard and asked to park the trailer in a specific location. Small RFID tags or GPS tracking devices may be affixed to trailers to track additional movement. The contents of the trailer are known through the previously transmitted ASN. When there is no urgent need to unload the trailer, it may remain in the yard for a prolonged period of time. The yard becomes an extension of the warehouse. Through the YMS, the WMS manages the inventory in the trailers. Since all movements are tracked, and the contents of trailers and containers are known, the inventory whereabouts are always accounted for. Yard jockeys, employees who move the trailers around the yard, are responsible for driving them to dock doors when messaged to do so. While this book focuses on automation technologies deployed within the four walls of a warehouse, it is important to understand the complexity of the yard itself. A YMS bridges the gap between the activities that take place outside the four walls with those that take place within them.

Dock scheduling also interacts with the internal resources deployed in the warehouse. Once trailers arrive at the dock, hydraulic dock technologies may be deployed to safely enable forklift trucks and other equipment to physically enter the trailer. After a trailer has been secured, the receiving processes formally commence and assigned personnel begin to unload the goods.

Truck Manifest Verification

Distribution Centers are on a continuous quest to improve traceability and accuracy. It is important to compare received goods against a purchase order and to record any discrepancies. A manifest is a physical document signed by a receiving party when goods arrive. It should match the data transmitted in the ASN. The manifest includes barcodes that identify each pallet, cases stacked on a pallet, and any parcels that have been loosely shipped. It also includes dimension and weight information of pallets, cases, packages, and individual items. To reduce downstream errors, the WMS should identify and report the discrepancies between the items contained on the purchase order from those appearing on the manifest or ASN. It must also record the associated item level detail to enable the automation of downstream processes.

Unloading Goods to the Staging Area

Forklift trucks are often used to unload pallets from trucks. Received pallets are scanned into inventory and moved to designated staging areas. Even in a fully manual warehouse, staging space needs to be carefully planned, with sufficient space allocated for temporary storage and for the movement of forklift trucks managing storage and retrieval tasks. When shipments don't arrive palletized, warehouse workers manually unload the individual cases or eaches, often utilizing a telescopic conveyor. Unloading jobs can be physically demanding and among the most unpleasant in a warehouse. Technologies exist to fully automate the process, for both pallet- and case-level loads, and can speed up the unloading process by an order of magnitude.

For pallet-level loads, several automated unloading options are available. Loads may be received as full or partial pallets and may be single- or multi-SKU. The same systems, known as Automated Truck Loading Systems (ATLS), are used for unloading and loading. According to Research and Markets, the Global ATLS market was approximately $2B in 2022, with an expected CAGR of seven percent through 2027. ATLS chain-based systems have two components that connect together. An active chain secured to the truck powers a passive chain that drives a conveyor on the dock.

With these systems, pallets can be unloaded from a truck in a matter of minutes. Since the trucks require modifications to interoperate with these systems, the option is viable when warehouse operators own their fleet of trucks. Extended fork systems also exist, which are capable of extracting slugs of pallets in a single shot, without any modification to the truck itself.

AGVs offer another option. When used for this purpose, they are programmed with multiple load retrieval patterns. Although they tend to be slower and more expensive than manual trucks, they are safer, operate more consistently, and reduce labor costs. The quality of the delivery trucks and the pallets can have a significant impact on the accessibility of the AGV and its retrieval capabilities. If the truck and the pallets are within acceptable tolerance levels, AGVs enter the truck and move pallets one by one to an inbound pallet conveyor or a temporary staging area.

Case-level automated truck unloading systems are more complicated, largely experimental, and are not widely deployed in production. They are designed differently from pallet-based systems. As an example, the Siemens RUBUS™ system requires a belt to be installed on the floor of the trailer. Utilizing the belts, loose-loaded parcels can be unloaded to connected conveyors and singulated in a matter of minutes. Robotic unloaders with suction-based end-effectors offer another option, capable of grabbing several cases at the same time and moving them onto inbound conveyors. Boston Dynamics is deploying its articulated arm robot named Stretch™, which consists of a suction-based gripper secured to an AMR. Guided by intelligent software and an integrated vision system, it grabs packages one by one and deposits them onto a powered, mobile conveyor that extends into the truck. Stretch™ can reportedly unload cases at a rate of 800 cases per hour. All options have pros and cons in relation to speed, flexibility, cost, dexterity, recoverability, and gentleness, with no technology yet emerging as a de facto leader.

Counting, Inspection, and the System of Record

In some environments, the physical counting of goods is deemed too labor intensive or costly to perform. It is assumed that the number of damaged, shorted, or unordered items is small enough, or the dollar value is low enough, that it doesn't warrant a verification process. In other environments, error rates are so high, or their impact so significant, that everything must be verified. Suppliers with poor track records are the ones most likely to have their products inspected before being accepted into inventory. In most cases, poor supplier performance levels result in financial penalties, which help to offset the cost of additional labor or automation. Bulk goods and goods with variable dimensions or weight (e.g., fresh food) also require inspection, to determine the precise dimensions or "catch weight" of the received products.

Damaged or unexpected goods are set aside, recorded as such, and prepared for shipment back to the supplier. When received goods are inspected, additional inventory information, such as serial numbers, expiration dates, and lot numbers, is captured for downstream use. Any discrepancy with the information on the truck manifest should be captured at this stage. Missing products or products shipped in excess are identified and recorded. Inspection and traceability are essential in industries like food, high-value electronics, and pharmaceuticals.

There are several technology options for automated and semiautomated inspection. Handheld laser scanners may be used to scan incoming items (pallets or cases), automatically reconciling them against the manifest. In high-throughput facilities, multisided barcode scanning tunnels or RFID portals may be used to identify packages at high speed, regardless of the position of the barcode on the package. Discrepancies are flagged and dealt with immediately. Mis-reads, incorrect labels, or damaged products may still result in inaccurate inventory levels or the wrong products being shipped.

Additional steps need to be taken to minimize the likelihood of errors, like automated scales to compare the weight of inbound pallets against the anticipated weights. When discrepancies are detected, manual intervention is required to determine the source of the issue. Each item can also be weighed and compared against its expected weight. Damaged goods may be detected using automated dimension checkers to identify package deformations.

When physical counting and verification are used, the WMS records items into inventory only after they are verified. Alternatively, inventory is updated based on the information in the manifest, with items that are later determined to be missing or damaged, adjusted in inventory. The earlier that product issues are detected in the cycle, the less costly it is for retailers and distributors. Shipping a defective product to a customer, managing the return, and reshipping a new product, is always the most expensive option. If received goods are unlabeled or unidentifiable upon receipt, new labels or tags are applied to enable them to be tracked by downstream processes. The equipment deployed is the same as the printing and labeling machines used to prepare packages or pallets for shipping.

Physical Inspection

All automated solutions have intrinsic error rates. When an issue is identified, a physical inspection is required to validate the finding and to determine the appropriate disposition. In some industries, statistical sampling is also performed, with random items being physically inspected at a configured frequency to ensure compliance with committed supplier specifications. Automated solutions will divert suspect or random goods to "hospital lanes" where employees rescan them and analyze the results on a screen. In the event of a fault, the error may be cleared and the product in question is reinducted into the system. If a minor issue is found (e.g., the foil wrap triggers a dimension check error), the issue can be repaired and the product or pallet re-scanned.

If there is a weight discrepancy, be it with a pallet or a case, a more in-depth process is used to determine the source of the issue. Items verified to be defective or received in error are routed to a staging area in preparation for return. The return reason is recorded by the WMS and printed out for each item in a shipment. The cost of the return is usually the responsibility of the supplier. Associated processing costs may be recovered through negotiated penalties, particularly when errors exceed contractually agreed upon thresholds.

RFID Tags

RFID tags are an alternative to barcodes. They can be affixed to products when they are accepted into inventory, be it at the pallet, case, or tote level. Passive tags do not contain powered transmitters as they simply reflect radio waves. They are inexpensive, typically costing less than $1 per unit, and enable inventory to be tracked actively as it is moved around a warehouse. Line of sight access is not required as it is with barcodes, enabling products stored in multiple depth locations to be tracked.

Drones and AMRs are becoming increasingly affordable technologies. They can read RFID tags by roaming a warehouse while transmitting radio waves, updating the WMS in real time with inventory information as it is reflected back to the reader. These solutions eliminate the need for costly and inaccurate cycle counting processes, where subsets of inventory are counted at designated intervals and compared against internal records, correcting any discrepancies.

Cross-Docking

Cross-docking operations transfer inbound goods to outbound shipments when they are received. Products are moved directly from receiving to shipping. As soon as inbound cases or pallets are scanned, the WMS or WES recognizes them as part of a cross-docking load. In an automated solution, a conveyor system, a high-speed sortation system, an AGV, or an AMR, is used to route the load to its shipping lane. The demand, the cut-off time, and the number of cross-docked items determine whether or not the transport speed should be adjusted to balance the arrival time, the energy efficiency, and the wear-and-tear of the equipment. Shipping labels are applied to all outbound loads as they head toward their respective shipping lanes. Some amount of cross-docking is managed in most distribution centers but it is used most frequently by parcel carriers like FedEx, UPS, and DHL.

The ROI

The more workers assigned to receiving, inspection, and cycle counting tasks, the easier it is to justify an automation investment in the receiving area. Most companies seek an ROI of three years or less, though in the case of larger and costlier deployments, the timeframe is often longer. In the case of receiving, the math is straightforward. Automation should reduce the number of shifts and limit the number of staff needed during each shift. Improved inventory accuracy may tip the scale further in favor of automation, as may the challenge of hiring workers, particularly for the most grueling or repetitive tasks.

Key Takeaways

- Receiving processes include dock-door assignment, manifest verification, product unloading, product verification, inventory receipts, product inspection, and disposition management.
- The yard, which is located outside the four walls of the warehouse, houses inventory in trailers that have yet to be unloaded. It is managed using a YMS.
- Advanced Shipping Notifications may be used to automatically identify discrepancies between products that were ordered and those that were delivered.
- There are a number of automated truck-unloading systems on the market for pallets. Automated truck unloading of cases is more complicated and most solutions remain limited to pilots, though robotic options are evolving and showing promise.

- Automated inbound product validation is partially achieved using electronic scales, scanning tunnels, and a WMS to identify weight and dimension discrepancies of received cases and pallets compared to what was expected.
- Not all inbound products in a distribution center require storage. Automated cross-docking transports inbound products directly from the receiving dock to the shipping dock, often using AGVs or AMRs.

CHAPTER 5

Automated Decanting and Storage

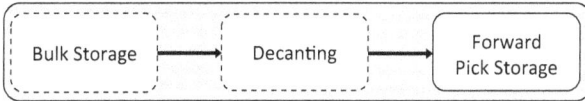

Many of us have experienced the impact of soaring real estate prices in recent years. The cost of land, particularly in more heavily populated urban areas, is at an all-time high. The challenge facing retailers and distributors who seek warehousing space is even higher. Not only must they contend with rising prices but they face increasing pressure to move their warehouses to more densely populated areas to minimize transportation costs and delivery times. Additionally, to meet customers' expectations, they are under pressure to store a wider array of goods than in the past. That means investing in larger warehouses, more frequent replenishment activities, or automation to make more efficient use of an existing space.

As discussed in Chapter 4, products are usually received in pallets or cases. In some industries, such as petroleum or lumber, they may be received in bulk, be it in liquid drums, in large sacks, in intermediate bulk containers (IBCs), or as building materials. Not all inbound products require storage as some may be cross-docked. In most industries, however, the majority of products are stored on pallets, in cases, or as eaches. They are usually decanted from the packaging in which they are received into a form suitable for short-term storage and picking.

Pallet Storage

Pallets may be stored in designated locations on the warehouse floor, in manual storage racks, or in an ASRS. Density, accessibility, and throughput are key factors in determining what type of storage is best suited for a particular operation. Warehouses often deploy different strategies for different products. Table 5.1 provides guidance on the best application of these alternatives:

Table 5.1 Relationship between density, accessibility, and throughput to help determine the most suitable warehouse storage approach

	Density	Accessibility	Throughput
Floor Storage	Low	High	Low
Storage Racks	Med-High	Med	Med
ASRS	High	Med-High	High

Pallet storage, with its high density of contained products, offers a lower cost of storage on a per-item level than case storage. It may be used for long-term (reserve) storage or for pallet-in/pallet-out material flow, when there is no need to alter the form of the pallets on shipment.

Floor Storage

Floor storage may be designed as a single layer, or pallets can be stacked on top of each other if the load capacities of the underlying pallets are able to withstand the weight of those above them. Stacking, particularly popular in the beverage industry, can double or triple the storage density but it lowers accessibility and throughput. While there is no racking cost, the overall cost per square foot of floor storage compared to racked storage is usually higher due to lower densities. Throughput when using floor storage tends to be quite low, given the broad storage area and the distance that must be traveled by fork trucks, AGVs, or AMRs as they transport pallets to various locations.

Pallet Rack Storage

There are a multitude of rack providers that offer both standard and custom rack configurations. The two main types of pallet racking systems used in warehouses are aisle-based systems, also known as Selective Racks, and high-density systems, known as Compact or Live Racks.

There are four types of selective racking: (1) wide aisle, (2) narrow aisle, (3) very narrow aisle (VNA), and (4) double deep. Warehouses must be designed for the required aisle widths that separate the racks to enable direct access to stored pallets. The maximum height of manual pallet racking solutions ranges between 10 and 15 meters, limited by the maximum reach of the forklift trucks that store and retrieve the pallets. VNA racking is usually at the higher end of the range. As the names suggest, aisle widths are successively reduced when moving from wide aisle systems (approximately four meters), to narrow aisle systems (approximately three meters), to very narrow aisle systems (approximately 1.5 meters). Aisle widths in double-deep systems are similar to those of wide aisle configurations but pallets are stored back-to-back, which serves to increase storage capacity by approximately 50 percent. The cost and complexity of forklift trucks tend to increase as aisle width decreases, with VNA trucks being the most advanced and expensive.

Compact and Live-racking systems sacrifice throughput in favor of density. They operate on either a first-in-first-out (FIFO) or a last-in-first-out (LIFO) basis. With Compact Racking, forklift trucks physically enter the internal aisles of the racks. With a FIFO method, the rack system is referred to as drive-through, as forklifts store products by accessing the rack on one side of the structure and retrieving them from the opposite side. With a LIFO method, the racking is referred to as drive-in, with forklifts being granted access only from one side, pushing older pallets deeper into the structure. Live-racking systems work similarly to FIFO systems, except that the pallets are stored on angled gravity rollers, eliminating the need for forklift trucks to physically enter the structure.

The true cost of racking is best calculated by storage location, typically ranging between $100 and $500 per location. The cost is impacted by the maximum height, the grade of steel, the load capacity, the configuration (e.g., single deep, double deep, multideep, and gravity), and seismic stability. Throughput rates tend to be higher than with floor storage solutions because the distance traveled is less. For example, in a 10-level racking system, the density may increase by an order of magnitude but the cost of Reach trucks or AGVs is much higher than that of standard forklift trucks.

Mole systems, which work hand-in-hand with forklifts, move pallets to and from storage locations in multideep configurations. They work collaboratively with high-reach trucks that move pallets vertically. These systems add considerable expense and are best compared against that of fully automated ASRS-based solutions.

In many manual warehouses, both Reach and Standard forklift trucks are used, with the former deployed in the racking area and the latter to transport pallets from one area to another.

No matter the choice, pallet racking is an expensive component of any warehouse, be it manual or automated. Making the right decision for a specific environment requires rigorous analysis and a key understanding of many parameters including SKU count, SKU turnover rate, throughput needs, SKU perishability, square footage, warehouse height, access to labor, capital budget, and so on. A good rule of thumb: the higher the density of a racking solution, the higher the capital cost outlay but the lower the associated labor costs.

Automated Pallet Storage

There are multiple automated options available for automated high bay storage and retrieval of pallets in a warehouse. Crane-based systems, known as Unit Loads, as shown in Figure 5.1, are the most common. They are arranged in aisles, with the cranes moving back and forth along a rail in each aisle. Load-handling carriers equipped with pallet forks are attached to the masts of the cranes. They are able to carry one or two pallets at a time, ascending and descending to the required height while the crane accelerates horizontally along its rail. Cranes use their pallet forks to store and retrieve pallets in single- or double-deep configurations. Unit Load ASRSs are able to store pallets as high as 50 meters in the air. They are designed with very narrow aisles, enabling storage densities to approach 90 percent of the available volume in deep lane configurations. Achievable densities reduce to approximately 75 percent in double deep configurations. Maximum load capacities vary but are typically around 1500 kg. Average storage and retrieval rates of 60 pallets in/out per hour are typical for each aisle. In multideep, mole-based configurations, the

Figure 5.1 A rendering of a 3-aisle Unit Load ASRS system with associated inbound/outbound conveyor. The crane accelerates horizontally along its rail while its load moves vertically on the mast. Double-deep or multideep storage configurations increase the density but reduce overall throughput. © 2023 by Dematic Corp

rates will be lower but the storage density higher. In single-deep configurations, the storage and retrieval rates are higher but the storage density is reduced due to increased aisle space.

Cranes are also compatible with powered moles that travel below the racks on each level. Moving perpendicular to the cranes, they are used to store and retrieve pallets deep into the racking structure. Similar to compact or live racking, moles increase the storage capacity but they come at a cost. They make sense to consider when a warehouse stores large numbers of identical products in back-to-back locations, particularly when storage space is at a premium, as in refrigerated or frozen warehouses.

An alternative to a Unit Load ASRS is a shuttle-based pallet system. With these systems, separate vertical lifts move pallets in or out, usually at the end of an aisle. Shuttles on each level move the pallets to and from the lift. Pallets are moved in and out of single deep storage locations with an extractor or conveyor affixed to the shuttle. In the case of multideep configurations, a detachable mole enters and exits the shuttle to pick up or drop off pallets. These systems offer increased parallelism as shuttles move concurrently. While higher throughput rates are achievable, the vertical speed of the single lift in each aisle, coupled with pallet handoff times, constrains the performance gains.

While shuttle-based pallet systems have their use cases, more often than not, the relatively modest pallet throughput requirements can be met with lower-priced crane-based solutions.

Case and Tote Storage

After inbound pallets have been received and potentially stored, they may be sent to a decanting area for depalletization and subsequent storage. In distribution centers, it is common for inbound products to be received in one form (e.g., pallets) and processed for shipping in a different form. As a prerequisite to downstream picking, products are stored in the form in which they are most likely to be fulfilled. In many industries, grocery distribution being an example, case-level picking is standard. In a large grocery distribution center, inbound products are received as homogeneous pallets and stored as such until they are needed to fulfill orders, at which time they are depalletized and stored as individual cases.

Pallets may be decanted manually or with an automated solution. Regardless of the approach, the WMS adjusts the inventory on hand to manage the correct unit of measure at all times. For example, one pallet containing 300 24-packs would be modified post depalletization to be 300 separately stored 24-packs.

While depalletizing, shrink-wrap is removed and pallets are broken down layer by layer. With automated systems, vacuum-based depalletizers are common, capable of removing a single layer of cases from a pallet in one shot. Layers are moved to a descrambling platform to spread the cases apart, enabling them to be transported in a single file after passing through a right-angle transfer on a conveyor line. Small cases may be placed into totes and suction-based grippers affixed to articulated arm robots may be used to automate the process.

Manual Case and Tote Storage

In manual warehouses, cases are stored in accessible bin locations or shelving units. Storage density tends to be relatively low but accessibility is high. Replenishment is often time consuming in a busy warehouse, as pickers and replenishers may get in each other's way, resulting in delays in accessing the bin locations.

Carton flow racks reduce accessibility to bins as it may be more challenging to reach the ones at the back of a rack. On the other hand, they increase the density of the storage space and speed up replenishment, which is done from the back side of the rack, avoiding congestion due to concurrent picking operations. These racks are commonly deployed in lightly automated, person-to-goods, pick-to-light, or pick-to-voice environments, designed with a variety of picking strategies.

Automated Case Storage Options

ASRSs that store totes and cases are sophisticated and varied. Some are designed strictly for tote storage. Others, most notably shuttle technologies, can efficiently store both cases and totes of varying dimensions. When measured at the unit level, case-level storage is more expensive than pallet storage but it reduces the access time of the cases and the throughput of orders. Because of this, automated case and tote-level storage is used for direct picking operations but typically not for long-term storage of goods.

Regardless of the type of ASRS, automated case storage significantly improves the density and throughput of a warehouse. When small packages or individual items are stored in totes, the items must first be decanted from the cases in which they were received. The process may be done manually by opening the cases and dropping the items into the totes, or with an automated decanting machine. Automated solutions precision-cut the received cases and empty their contents, either in bulk by flipping the cases to release the items onto a descrambling conveyor, or one-by-one with an articulated arm robot. The individual items are then moved into a tote. The WES records the identifier (license plate) of the totes and the relevant SKU details (e.g., lot numbers) of the items deposited into them, while decrementing the number of cases that previously contained the items. The totes are moved to a storage location determined by the WES and the items are marked as being available to fulfill orders.

Vertical and horizontal carousels were introduced in the 1950s. They are often used to store products that occupy a relatively small space. They are usually configured in pods with each operator assigned to two or three pods. Vertical lift modules are similar to vertical carousels but use a lift mechanism rather than a circular chain to move the internal shelving units. Vertical buffer modules are self-enclosed storage systems that operate like crane-based systems but in a more compact configuration.

Mini Load cranes, which are like Unit Load cranes, have advantages over carousels and vertical lift modules in that they utilize the full height and footprint of a warehouse and can store a wider range of products. Shuttle systems (e.g., Dematic Multishuttle) and robotic cube systems (e.g., AutoStore) were released in the 2000s. They offer higher throughput, more flexible configurations, less downtime, and improved sequencing. When automating large distribution centers with a large number of SKUs and high pick rates, shuttles and cube systems are the most popular. Their one-time cost is quite high but given their speed, density, and efficiency, they often offer the lowest cost solution when measured on a per storage location or per pick basis.

Mini Load Systems

Mini Load ASRSs, as shown in Figure 5.2, are designed and manufactured by multiple leading automation vendors and integrators. They were first released in the 1980s and work similarly to Unit Load ASRSs but their load-handling mechanisms and weight capacities are different. Racks and shelves must be precision built to conform to a crane's exacting specifications. A single crane travels back and forth on rails along each aisle with its carriage ascending and descending on a mast until its load-handling device (LHD) is positioned adjacent to its target location. LHDs are telescoping arms with the ability to grasp multiple load sizes. Cranes may be configured with single or dual masts and most support multiple LHD on a single mast to improve throughput. Single-mast cranes have the ability

Figure 5.2 A Dematic Mini Load system configured with a racking system that extends to the ceiling of a warehouse, showing its extremely narrow aisle widths. © 2023 by Dematic Corp

to mount multiple LHDs vertically, one above the other, while dual-mast cranes, which support increased heights, mount their LHDs beside each other. Each LHD can typically support loads of about 250 kg. Their speed and acceleration can yield presentation rates up to 300 cases or totes per hour. Aisle widths may be as narrow as 36 inches. Mini Loads are best suited to warehouses that store a large number of relatively slow-moving products, where storage density is prioritized over throughput.

Automated Shuttle Systems

Shuttle systems were popularized by Dematic in the latter part of the 2000s with the release of its first generation Multishuttle. Most leading automation integrators now offer similar systems as a foundation of their high-end solutions. One or more vertical lifts transport loads to multiple storage levels. Shuttles, powered by bus bars or batteries, travel at high speed, storing and retrieving goods from rack locations adjacent to each aisle. They have telescopic extractors which enable them to access multideep storage locations. Data and control signals are sent to each shuttle either wirelessly or via a bus bar. The primary advantage of a shuttle system over a Mini Load ASRS is concurrency. Products can be transported at the same time on multiple levels within the same aisle. The factor that limits throughput the most in a shuttle system is lift speed, which is why some implementations deploy multiple lifts per aisle (known as drive-through configurations), at the expense of some storage density.

In most cases, each level within each aisle has a single, dedicated shuttle but some manufacturers offer roaming (or 2D) shuttles, enabling them to service multiple aisles. Multiple shuttles per aisle are also possible. Dematic's solution uses a proprietary inter-aisle transfer mechanism, constraining each shuttle to a single aisle but enabling them to transfer stored products from one aisle to the next. Roaming shuttles add complexity and cost to each unit but enable enhanced scalability and reduced downtime. Three-dimensional shuttles, which reduce or eliminate the need for lifts are also available from some vendors and are designed to travel both horizontally and vertically.

Most shuttle solutions can store and retrieve loads of different dimensions which increases density. The primary advantage of shuttles over Mini Loads is parallelism, enabling them to more easily sequence cases and totes in a precise order as they travel toward pick stations.

Figure 5.3 A Dematic multishuttle 2 system showing storage of both totes and cases of varying sizes. Each level in an aisle is serviced by a dedicated shuttle. © 2023 by Dematic Corp

Load capacities of shuttles are typically about 50 kg, which is significantly lower than Mini Loads. Horizontal speeds are in the 4 to 5 m/s range, with accelerations of 2 m/s^2. There is no theoretical limit on the height of a shuttle system, although installations rarely exceed 40 levels. Aisles can be of varying heights, enabling a system to conform to the contours of an existing building. Tote and case presentation rates of 600 per hour are achievable, making shuttle technology well suited for use in high throughput, high-density environments. An example of a multiaisle shuttle system with custom racking and associated inbound and outbound conveyors is shown in Figure 5.3.

Robotic Cube Storage

Robotic cube systems, as depicted in Figure 5.4, offered by AutoStore and Ocado, have become popular with customers because of their unique advantages. While they support only tote storage, they offer unmatched storage density, particularly for brownfield projects where ceiling heights are often limited. A grid system is erected to conform to the contours

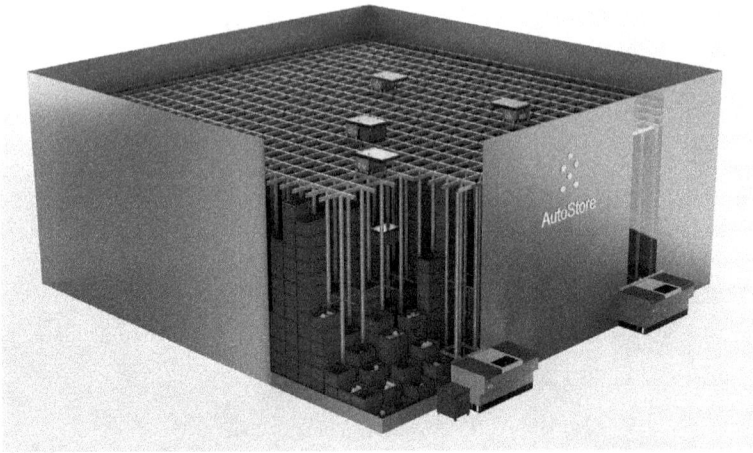

Figure 5.4 Schematic of an AutoStore grid equipped with 4 pick stations. © 2023 by AutoStore holdings

of the space, enabling efficient use of irregularly shaped areas. Totes are stacked directly on top of each other within the grid, with very little space separating adjacent totes. The top of the grid must be flat as bots travel on the surface in both directions, with access to all locations. Multiple tote sizes are supported but all totes in a particular deployment must be of the same size. When larger totes are used, fewer layers are supported than with smaller totes. In either case, the maximum height of the grid is approximately six meters.

Software directs each radio-controlled robot to retrieve totes from the top of the grid and to transport them to lifts. When a targeted tote is below the surface, the robot digs it out with a telescopic LHD, moving higher totes to neighboring locations. The slotting is self-optimizing, with fast movers naturally ascending to the top of the grid and slow movers naturally descending to the bottom. One of the strengths of the approach is its scalability. When more throughput is required, it's easy to add more robots to the system, though traffic congestion eventually becomes a limiting factor. When a robot fails, it can be removed without affecting other robots and the system slows down only proportionally. Subsequent tasks are redirected by the control software in real time to the active robots. Replenishment and order picking rates may be slightly below that of shuttle systems but cube systems support higher densities, superior scalability, and fewer single points of failure. They cannot, however, ascend as high as many alternative solutions. Robotic cube systems are used across multiple industries including grocery, retail, 3PL, and healthcare.

Other Alternatives

While Mini Loads, shuttles, and robotic cubes are popular, there are some other alternatives worthy of consideration. Exotec is growing in popularity with its scalable SkyPod system, shown in Figure 5.5. It uses ground-based robots that ascend vertically into a rack, eliminating the need for separate lifts, shuttles, or conveyors.

Companies like Alert Innovation, Symbotic, OPEX, and Attabotics, also offer multidimensional shuttle solutions with a number of flexibility and scalability advantages. Reel-in Robotics, shown in Figure 5.6, uses cable-driven robots to store and retrieve loads of varying sizes and weights. They offer an innovative alternative to traditional ASRS machines, which can be configured to work with preexisting racking structures.

Figure 5.5 Exotec's Skypod system, showing multiple Skypods within the racking structure. After retrieving a designated tote, the bots exit the rack and deliver the totes to dedicated picking stations. © 2023 by Exotec

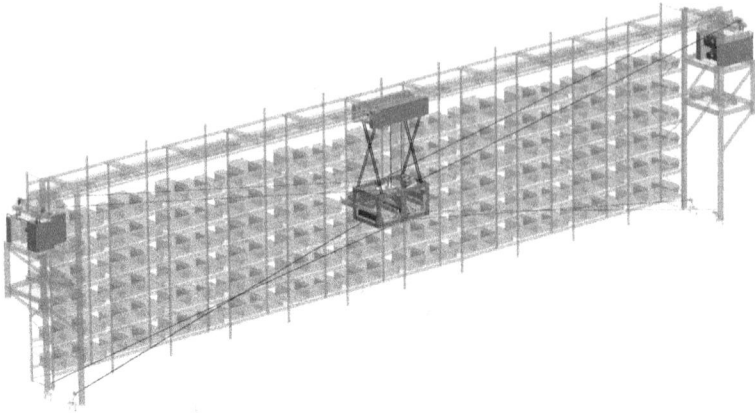

Figure 5.6 Reel-in Robotics' CableBot solution. © 2023 by Reel-in Robotics

Lift mechanisms on AMRs also offer storage and retrieval capabilities at moderate heights, which is changing the competitive landscape. RoboShuttle from Geek+ and HaiPick from Hai Robotics, shown in Figure 5.7, are two such examples, each capable of accessing products stored in racks up to 8 meters in height. Their movement is managed using the same orchestration engine as the other robots in their fleet. While they can't ascend to the same heights as Mini Load or shuttle systems, they are more portable and scalable, and they are easier to deploy.

Initially popularized by the apparel industry, pouch-based systems, as shown in Figure 5.8, offer yet another storage alternative. They are combination storage, conveyance, and sortation systems, affixed to the ceiling of warehouses to conserve floor space. Smaller items, typically less than 3 kg, are dropped into pouches upon receipt, with each SKU being mapped to a corresponding pouch identifier. Each pouch can hold a single SKU that may be manually or automatically inducted or removed. When idle, the pouches can be squeezed together to conserve space. Using intelligent routing and clever software, products may be retrieved and sequenced from any location in any order. The technology is particularly useful for returns management as returned products can be assigned to new orders immediately after validation.

Case and item storage are at the heart of many automated warehouses and the associated technologies tend to be among the most expensive.

Figure 5.7 HaiPick from Hai Robotics. © 2023 by Hai Robotics

There is an ever-increasing number of technology options, all with pros and cons that should be carefully considered. If raw performance is paramount, shuttle systems may be the best choice. If storage density is most important, it's hard to beat a cubic solution. If a warehouse has

Figure 5.8 Pouch sorter from Dematic. © 2023 by Dematic Corp

limited unused floorspace, a pouch solution may be the right answer. If flexibility and scalability are critical, an AMR-based solution may be the right choice. When looking for the best compromise, a multidimensional robotic solution should be investigated. More often than not, multiple simulations should be developed and compared to determine which technology can best achieve specific requirements.

Key Takeaways

- Pallets can be stored on the floor of a warehouse, in storage racks, or in a Unit Load ASRS. Density of storage and throughput tends to increase with the level of automation.
- Pallet racking is designed using a variety of aisle widths and configurations, including wide-aisle, narrow-aisle, very-narrow-aisle, and double-deep.
- Unit Load cranes form the basis of most pallet-based ASRS systems though shuttle-based systems offer advantages in certain situations.

- A wide variety of automated case and tote storage solutions are on the market including shuttle systems, carousels, Mini Load ASRSs, cubic systems, AMR-based solutions, and multidimensional shuttles.
- Pouch-based storage offers the advantage of managing storage, conveyance, and sortation in a single system. It is particularly popular in the apparel industry and can be effective in simplifying the returns process.

CHAPTER 6

Automated Order Picking and Replenishment

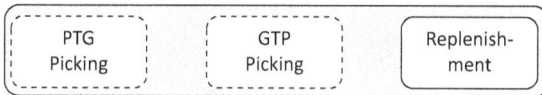

PTG Picking	GTP Picking	Replenish-ment

The first warehouses were pure storage facilities but over time as they evolved into modern distribution centers, much of their value shifted toward order fulfillment. Efficient order picking and replenishment became critical in order to maximize accuracy and throughput.

It is useful to recall Figure 2.2 in Chapter 2 that highlights different warehouse environments and technologies as they are particularly relevant to order picking and replenishment. For order picking, these business demands map to specific modes of operation and technologies as shown in Figure 6.1.

Person-to-Goods Order Picking

Basic Person-to-Goods

Person-to-Goods picking is performed by pickers walking to inventory locations and depositing goods into a tote, similar to how a grocery shopper uses a well-organized shopping list to efficiently move through a supermarket. For the simplest warehouses (lower left quadrant in the diagram), this is exactly how picking operates, except that the "shopping lists" for the pickers are generated by the warehouse management system. For more complex warehouses, pickers receive their instructions through a pick-to-light system, voice headsets, or RF terminals.

A picker may be picking a single order or a set of orders, depositing items into multiple totes. All totes are housed in a wheeled cart that is

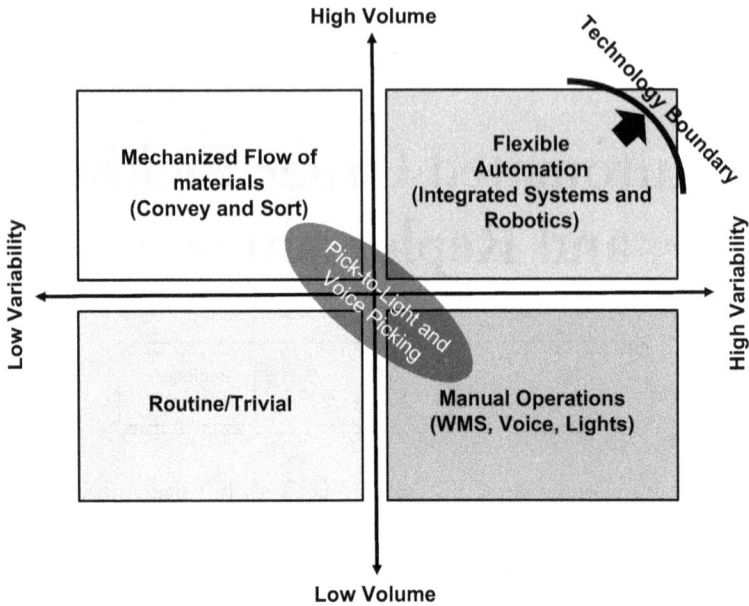

Figure 6.1 Key picking technologies for different business demands

pushed along as picking progresses. Completed pick totes corresponding to a single, complete order go directly to packing and shipping. Otherwise, they are sent to a consolidation station to assemble the final order packages.

PTG picking processes are relatively simple to implement, require limited capital, and enable efficient storage and space utilization because of the dexterity and intelligence of human pickers. They can reach tight spaces, validate products, and open cartons or pallets to access goods as necessary. The flexibility of human pickers also enables these systems to react to changes in the warehouse, including changing workloads or order types. The order fulfillment lead time is relatively short for simple order picking, though subject to high variability, which limits the service level that the warehouse can commit to. An example of a simple pick-to-light PTG solution, with items deposited into order cases being pushed along a manual conveyor, is shown in Figure 6.2. For a modest investment, significant efficiency gains can be achieved with solutions of this nature when compared against manual, printed pick-list-based operations.

On the other hand, PTG systems have relatively low productivity rates (typically less than 200 picks per hour) and suffer from human

Figure 6.2 Simple manual conveyor-based pick-to-light, PTG solution from Matthews Automation. © 2023 by Matthews Automation Solutions

errors which reduce picking accuracy. Multiple-order picking increases throughput at the cost of extended lead times because all orders conclude only after the last one is done and consolidation is complete.

The start and end of each cycle, transporting completed pick totes or carts, and picking up empty totes all contribute to the reduced productivity of basic PTG operations. AMRs, acting as self-directed carts, such as the one shown in Figure 6.3, can eliminate the need for a picker to travel back and forth to the delivery point. When properly integrated into the picking operation, AMR systems can detect when order totes near completion. They can be ready and waiting with a replacement vehicle, just in time to ensure uninterrupted order picking.

Zone Picking

While zone picking falls under the umbrella of Person-to-Goods operations, it is different enough in its operation to merit a separate description. It divides warehouses into separate "zones," each storing different SKUs. Picking an order is not assigned to a single picker, but its items are divided into groups, with each group corresponding to a different zone. Zone picking can be performed sequentially using a "pick-and-pass" process, where an order tote travels from one zone to the next, serviced by dedicated pickers in each zone. Alternatively, the orders can

Figure 6.3 AMR-assisted Person-to-Goods picking using PickPal from Tompkins Robotics. © 2023 by Tompkins Robotics

be processed in parallel, with all items in an order being picked simultaneously into different totes. The totes are then sent to a consolidation area (e.g., a Put Wall) where the final orders are assembled from the contents of the received totes. In this case, it is possible for items corresponding to multiple orders to arrive at the consolidation station in the same tote, which increases the overall throughput. The transport of the picked totes between zones or between the picking zone and the consolidation area can be done manually by pickers, via pick-to-conveyor, or via AMRs.

The choice of the transportation method depends on the required throughput and the variability of the operation. Manual transfer is the slowest but it maximizes flexibility. Conveyor-based transport has a higher capital cost and the highest throughput, but it has the least flexibility (e.g., redefining zones in a warehouse would require expensive modification of the installed conveyor layout). AMRs lie somewhere in the middle, offering increased flexibility and higher throughput than manual operations but lower throughput than conveyor systems. A summary of the various PTG methodologies is shown in Table 6.1.

Table 6.1 Summary of Person-to-Goods methodologies

		Assigned pickers	
		One	Many
Orders picked at a time	One	Simple order picking with paper, pick-to-light, and voice picking. Lowest throughput.	Zone picking: Pick and pass with manual, conveyor, or AMR transfer between zones.
	Many	Batch or wave picking with carts or AMRs.	Zone picking with consolidation areas (e.g., Put Walls). Use of pick-to-conveyor for transportation.

Evolution of Person-to-Goods Picking

The emergence of e-commerce created a need for fast order fulfillment, high throughput, and a large number of inventory SKUs. Additionally, e-commerce fulfillment facilities must adapt their throughput levels to match demand conditions. This has driven additional innovation in Person-to-Goods systems. Improvements are possible across three dimensions:

- Reduce unproductive walk time: Introducing AMRs that follow the picker and self-dispatch when the orders are full, with an empty replacement AMR ready to pick up where the last one left off.
- Eliminate batch and wave inefficiencies: Planned batches and waves have inherent inefficiencies due to the natural variability in picking operations and, in the case of e-commerce, a continuous stream of orders arriving at the fulfillment center. A modern WES can operate in a waveless fashion, releasing orders to the pickers as soon as capacity becomes available, without the need to wait for the batch

or wave to complete. The software is able to select which orders to release based on the resources that become available and their real-time location in the warehouse.

- Minimize the travel distance between picks: Use real-time information on the status of the order-picking process and the location of each picker to assign and reassign picks to different workers. A WES, with access to the real-time picker and inventory information, is able to insert a picking operation on the fly as a new order is released, as new inventory becomes available, or if a worker misses a pick.

The common thread is the role that an integrated WES plays in directing the operations. A state-of-the-art WES differentiates itself from a WCS or WMS through its access to real-time execution information, order demand information, real-time task assignments, and sophisticated optimization algorithms. This level of integrated functionality is largely unavailable in traditional WMS/WCS split systems which often suffer from bottlenecks in automated fulfillment operations.

Goods-to-Person

In contrast to PTG, GTP systems move goods in inventory to a stationary picker. These systems rely on more sophisticated automation than PTG systems as they cannot utilize the spatial awareness of the picker to locate the inventory. GTP systems must manage multiple material handling processes to support a sustained order fulfillment flow in a facility, like the one depicted in Figure 6.4.

The core picking functions in a GTP environment are:

- Locate and retrieve the required inventory from storage
- Transport and route the inventory to the assigned picker
- Present the goods to the picker, together with the associated picking instructions
- Dispatch, transport, and route the order totes to order consolidation or packing stations

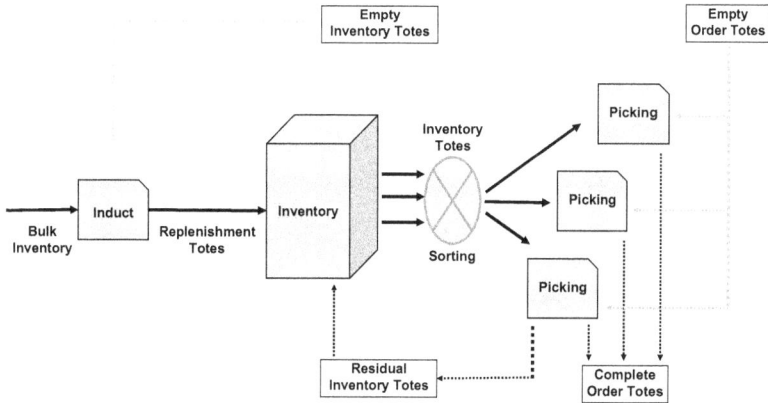

Figure 6.4 Material flows in Goods-to-Person fulfillment

Automation requires additional functions to be performed in order to operate reliably and continuously:

- Identification and induction of inventory into storage
- Tracking of available inventory and storage locations
- Verifying the result of pick operations
- Returning unused inventory to storage
- Replenishing inventory totes when their item count falls below a predetermined threshold
- Handling of inventory totes that are emptied as a result of picking operations
- Supplying order totes as required by the picking operation

Most GTP configurations use pre-existing subsystems for their main functions, tightly integrated to maximize the utilization of space and to minimize inventory travel time. Automation vendors also incorporate auxiliary functions in their integrated solutions, such as integrating routing conveyors and replenishment stations with storage and pick stations.

Location and Retrieval of Inventory

Since a picker cannot approach, identify, or acquire goods from a static inventory location in a GTP solution, the automation system must provide active storage and equipment to select and move the goods. Inventory is usually stored in standardized totes or trays specifically designed for the storage system.

In some applications, like grocery dry goods, packaged goods may be handled directly, eliminating the cost of totes or trays and allowing for denser storage. The downside is that inconsistent or damaged packaging often leads to a greater number of faults which require manual intervention to repair and clear.

The technology required for GTP operations is the same as the technology described in Chapter 5, but it must be optimized for speed of retrieval. The four most common types of case/tote storage used are as follows:

- Mini Load cranes, which offer the lowest cost per unit of storage but have relatively low throughput.
- Shuttle systems, offering very high throughputs but limited density and relatively high costs to install and operate.
- Cubic systems, which maximize density in lower ceiling height environments while offering throughputs that approach shuttle systems.
- Pouch or garment-on-hanger storage for specialized applications, mainly in the apparel industry.

Transport and Routing

Totes retrieved from storage are routed to pick locations through a fixed infrastructure of conveyors and sorters, or using a fleet of small autonomous robots, each transporting a single tote from the storage outlet to the pick station.

Present and Dispatch

The purpose of GTP systems is to provide a continuous stream of work to pickers, minimizing distractions on unproductive tasks. The pick station is the focal point of the operation, where inventory and orders come together and goods are transferred between inventory totes and order totes.

Once the inventory totes arrive at the picking station, they are presented to the picker with instructions on the operation at hand. These pick stations vary in sophistication and ergonomics, from simple platforms where the conveyor system moves the tote to ergonomic stations with rapid tote exchangers that can reach up to 1,000 picks per hour.

The core functions of the pick station are:

- Present goods to be picked from inventory to the picker
- Present containers or totes to place the goods
- Provide instructions to the picker on the specific action to perform
- Receive input from the picker on the completion of the operation, including any deviations or exceptions

Typically, goods are presented sequentially to the picker, synchronized with picking instructions. The picker remains stationary as instructions are presented on a large display attached to the station, often with pictures and other multimedia elements. One operation at a time is presented, with the order of operations determined by the controlling software system. Pick stations may have one or multiple order tote positions, enabling the picker to fulfill multiple orders simultaneously.

Single-order stations are ergonomically optimized, with carefully designed dimensions and adjustable settings to suit the preferences of individual pickers. These stations support the highest pick rates and the shortest lead times for single orders, important metrics for e-commerce operations. The sequencing of inventory totes to stations is a critical function of the controlling software. An out-of-order tote may not only impair the fulfillment of one order but a whole sequence of orders. In larger operations, it is often necessary to install additional material handling equipment to buffer and resequence totes that would otherwise arrive out of order. These are small-capacity automated storage units unto themselves.

Multiorder pick stations, such as the one shown in Figure 6.5, require less strict tote sequencing as goods associated with any of the active orders can be processed in the next operation. These stations offer lower ergonomic optimization and pick rates, however, requiring the picker to stretch to more distant order tote locations, increasing the probability of errors.

Figure 6.5 Four-order, high-speed pick station from Dematic.
© 2023 by Dematic Corp

The picker acknowledges the completion of an operation directly on the screen or by depressing a physical button adjacent to each order tote. Advanced vision systems may also be deployed to recognize the completion of a pick without any operator intervention, providing additional validation of the accuracy of the operation.

The control software must keep track of an order's completion and then trigger the movement of the associated tote, either in an automated fashion or by instructing the picker to move the completed tote to an outbound transport mechanism (usually a conveyor). Auxiliary systems retrieve empty totes for new orders with varying levels of automation. It may be a manual system where the operator picks a tote from a stack, scans it for association with the new order, and places it in the pick station. Alternatively, it may be a fully automated feeder system that performs the same functions in an automated way.

Inventory totes, once the picking operation is complete, are removed from the pick station and either returned to storage if they contain residual inventory or routed to decanting/replenishment stations for refilling and reinsertion into the system.

Mobile Inventory Systems

The previous sections focused on the most common GTP systems, with a clear separation of responsibilities between storage, transport, and presentation. An alternative system pioneered by Kiva Systems (acquired by Amazon in 2012) uses passive storage racks and a fleet of robot carriers. Robots travel between the storage area and the picking stations, combining the storage, movement, and presentation functions. These systems do have some limitations:

- Spatial density is limited by the height that pickers can reach.
- Picker productivity is lower compared with that of ergonomic pick stations.
- Throughput is sensitive to congestion in the picking area, with potential "traffic jams" of robots as they head toward pickers, more pronounced as the number of line items per order increases.
- Storage density and retrieval speeds are a trade-off. To ensure fast retrieval, racks must be organized along access lanes to minimize or eliminate rack shuffling, clearing the path for retrieval of the target inventory.

Despite the above limitations, mobile systems of this nature have many advantages and are becoming increasingly popular in e-commerce environments with large variations in SKUs or seasonal patterns. They are relatively quick to deploy, they scale effectively within the bounds of their limiting constraints, and they can overcome some of their limitations when coupled with sophisticated scheduling and routing software.

Ancillary Functions

The smooth operation of a GTP system relies on accurate inventory data as soon as orders need to be fulfilled. These systems need to perform a set of ancillary functions to ensure that inventory counts are always correct.

The WES or WCS needs to keep track of the quantity and location of inventory in order to dispatch the right tasks in the right order to the storage engine, be it a shuttle system, a swarm of bots, or a cubic system. It also needs to identify the goods that need to be replenished and on what timelines. When the need to initiate replenishment has been identified, the replenishment subsystem needs to be activated. This can be supported by using the same pick stations running in reverse or with dedicated stations provisioned to induct new inventory totes into the system.

When a picking operation is complete, inventory totes with residual inventory are routed back to an available storage location. Depleted inventory totes are rerouted to induction or decanting stations for reuse, and order totes are routed to order consolidation or packing stations.

Order totes are often validated after the pick operation is complete. A simple way to do this is to compare the weight of the order tote with its expected weight, based on information maintained by the WES. Totes that are not within an acceptable tolerance level are routed to an exception handling area for further inspection. If this is not possible (e.g., products differentiated by color), a visual inspection check, either by operators or by vision systems, may be conducted before the order is packaged and prepared for shipping.

Robotic Picking

The picking methods described in the previous sections all optimize picking by minimizing or eliminating nonproductive tasks. Until recently, the inherent capabilities of human pickers, including the accuracy of hand-eye coordination and the dexterity of human hands, exceeded the capabilities of automated technologies. This is changing as a number of technology startups and research divisions within large retailers and systems integrators have invested in the design of robotic manipulation and artificial vision systems. Robotic solutions rely heavily on advancements in machine learning (ML) and artificial intelligence (AI) that enable more adaptable algorithms to be implemented. In late 2022, Amazon Robotics announced the early deployment of a robotic piece-picking cell with artificial vision to guide an articulated arm. Over the past five years, established automation vendors such as Dematic, Bastian, and Daifuku

Figure 6.6 A GTR picking cell developed by Covariant, shown picking items from arriving donor totes and depositing them into a Put Wall. © 2023 by Covariant

have been deploying pilot installations of Goods-to-Robot (GTR) picking cells. Specialized vendors like Covariant, shown in Figure 6.6, actively compete in this space, often through strategic partnerships with leading integrators. They offer intelligent, cloud-based software, deep learning technologies, and innovative robotic manipulators to pick a wide array of items with unprecedented accuracy.

Robot-to-Goods (RTG) technologies, like the one from Brightpick shown in Figure 6.7, are also beginning to enter the market. The unstructured environment in which the robot operates increases the complexity of the problem space. Brightpick, with its Autopicker solution, simplifies the complexity by retrieving both order and donor totes onto the AMR and moving items from the donor tote to the order tote using a mounted robotic arm. When the picks from the order tote are complete, the AMR returns it to storage.

In addition to the traditional image of the articulated arm robot, there are specialized applications of robotic technology for mixed case palletizing that have been successfully deployed in grocery and consumer packaged goods distribution centers. In these cases, a robot manipulator horizontally pushes cases into position on each layer of a pallet, abiding

Figure 6.7 Autopicker from Brightpick. © 2023 by Photoneo Brightpick Group

by strict sequencing and stacking rules. Once a layer is full, the pallet is automatically lowered to the correct height, enabling the robot to begin filling the next layer.

Key Takeaways

- Picking is the central process that delivers fulfillment value in a warehouse.
- Depending on the volume and variability of the warehouse operation, picking processes are broadly classified as Person-To-Goods or Goods-To-Person, depending on whether the operator or the goods are moving to complete the picking operation.
- The focus of automation has been on minimizing the movement of operators to maximize the time they spend on the actual task of picking.
- Full automation of picking processes remains a challenge despite recent advances in vision and robotics. Newer systems are showing significant signs of improvement through the use of machine learning and artificial intelligence.

CHAPTER 7

Order Consolidation, Packing, and Value-Added Services

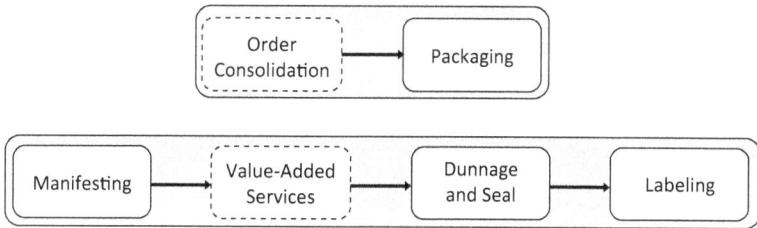

```
┌─────────────────────────────────────────────┐
│  ┌ ─ ─ ─ ─ ─ ┐                               │
│  :   Order   :  ───────▶  ┌──────────────┐   │
│  : Consolidation :        │  Packaging   │   │
│  └ ─ ─ ─ ─ ─ ┘            └──────────────┘   │
└─────────────────────────────────────────────┘

┌────────────────────────────────────────────────────────────────────┐
│ ┌──────────┐    ┌ ─ ─ ─ ─ ─ ┐    ┌──────────┐    ┌──────────┐        │
│ │Manifesting│──▶ : Value-Added :─▶│ Dunnage  │──▶ │ Labeling │        │
│ └──────────┘    :  Services  :    │ and Seal │    └──────────┘        │
│                 └ ─ ─ ─ ─ ─ ┘     └──────────┘                        │
└────────────────────────────────────────────────────────────────────┘
```

Imagine going to the supermarket to shop for multiple households at the same time using a single grocery cart. Would you navigate your way through the aisles several times or, if you had room, would you drop all the items into a single cart and consolidate them later? In most cases, you would likely do the latter.

A warehouse is similar. As the number of orders being processed increases, it usually makes sense to maximize the pick rate at the expense of an additional consolidation step. Several options are available.

Consolidation Stations

A consolidation station offers an effective, low-cost solution for PTG environments, particularly when orders are released in small batches. The WES tracks the status of batched orders as they are being picked. Picked items may belong to any order in the batch, and they may be commingled in the same tote with items from other orders. When the software detects that a sufficient number of orders have been picked, the associated totes are sent to a consolidation station. While there are remaining orders in the batch that require further picking, filled totes containing items for those orders circulate on a buffer conveyor. They are only released to the consolidation station when the orders in the batch containing those items have been fully picked. The WES is responsible for directing the totes as efficiently as possible to consolidation stations by minimizing the number of times they need to be moved back to the buffer conveyor.

Workers are assigned to one of multiple consolidation stations. The stations contain the equipment and accessories required to package the order including the monitors that display the instructions, cardboard shipping boxes, and filling material (dunnage). The size of the cardboard shipping box to be used is displayed on the monitor after which it is selected and erected by the worker.

Consolidation Using Unit Sorters

Unit sorters, discussed in more detail in Chapter 8, may also be used for consolidation. They are particularly useful when large numbers of batch-picked items are included in each order. Picked items are sent to a unit sorter via a conveyor line. If the items are in totes, they are removed manually or with articulated arm robots before being inducted. Whether a split-tray, a tilt-tray, or a crossbelt, all unit sorters are composed of individual cells. Each cell transports a single item. Upon induction, items are scanned to identify their respective destination chutes. The sorter moves at high speed and when a particular cell reaches its destination, it fires by opening, tilting, or conveying its package down its designated chute. An example of a crossbelt sorter is shown in Figure 7.1. If a chute is not ready for an item, perhaps because the container is full, the item circulates on the sorter until the container is emptied and is ready to receive new items. Filled containers are packed out and prepared for shipping.

Consolidation Using Pouch Sorters

Pouch Sorter consolidation is unique as it does not require external conveyance or a picking system. Pouch Sorters are an all-in-one storage, conveyance, sortation, and consolidation solution. Perhaps their most distinctive feature is the matrix sortation algorithm. Items can be stored

Figure 7.1 A dual-sided crossbelt sorter from Dematic. © 2023 by Dematic Corp

throughout the warehouse, each dropped into a pouch and conveyed to a random location. All pouches are connected to a single overhead rail system. Orders are picked in batches and may include items from any area of the warehouse. All items in a given batch are moved to a special sortation buffer, also known as a dynamic buffer. The dynamic buffer can induct hundreds of pouches and through a three-stage cycle, the matrix sortation algorithm consolidates orders in perfect sequence, regardless of the number of orders or the number of items contained in each order. The solution is well-suited for e-commerce environments where there are a large number of orders, each with relatively few items. Once sorted, all pouches are sent to a pack station where their items can be manually or automatically unloaded into shipping containers.

Consolidation Using Put Walls

The most popular consolidation approach, especially in PTG environments, is a Put Wall. Put Walls resemble a set of mail slots, typically open on both sides. The WES controls the associated lighting system, with a set of lights installed adjacent to each slot (or cubby). There may be multiple Put Walls in a distribution or fulfillment center and each may have cubbies of varying sizes to accommodate bigger orders or larger items. Two workers are assigned to each Put Wall, one on the "put" side and one on the "pack" side. The approach works particularly well in e-commerce environments where the physical number of items per order is usually small (e.g., electronics, health and beauty, apparel, and small consumer packaged goods).

Items arrive at a Put Wall, like the one shown in Figure 7.2, in no particular sequence, often spread across multiple totes. The worker on the put-side inducts the tote by scanning its license plate, informing the WES that the tote has arrived at the consolidation station. The worker then scans each item individually, sending its associated SKU data to the WES, which uses it to identify the assigned cubby by illuminating its light. The worker deposits the item into the cubby and depresses the button to inform the WES that the put-operation is complete. The worker repeats the process for each item in the tote until it is empty. The empty tote is then moved to a designated area, where it is stacked until it is retrieved for a new batch-pick operation. The process continues as successive totes are inducted into the Put Wall by the put-side worker. After all items in an order have been put into their designated slot, a light on the pack side of the wall is illuminated by the WES. This signals the pack-side operator that the order is complete and ready to be packed out into a shipping carton.

There are many shapes, sizes, and variations of Put Walls. With configurable Put Walls, the pack-out step may be avoided altogether. Shipping cartons are placed directly onto associated shelving units, adjacent to corresponding lights. The put operation works the same way but in this case, the pack operator is responsible for labeling and removing the shipping carton, and for replacing it with a new carton.

While Put Walls are straightforward in concept, the associated WES algorithms are quite complex. For the consolidation process to work efficiently, the WES must ensure that there are no bottlenecks, that all Put Walls are equally busy, that the right slot and carton size are selected for each order, and that all items associated with an order arrive at the Put Wall within a defined time window. It must also be able to locate missing

Figure 7.2 A put wall from Matthews automation, with an illuminated light identifying the slot where the current item is to be placed. © 2023 by Matthews Automation Solutions

items and diagnose problems as they occur, such as when required items don't arrive by the required cutoff time.

Put Wall technology has advanced over the last decade. OPEX Corporation, for example, introduced an automated Put Wall solution named SureSort in 2017 which automatically sorts items into order totes using a configurable number of internal, multidirectional bots.

Consolidation of Mixed-Case Pallets

Not all consolidation techniques use strict "pick then consolidate" processes. For example, mixed case palletizing, used heavily in the grocery industry, takes a two-phase approach to picking and consolidation.

As products are needed to fulfill orders, homogenous pallets are retrieved from long-term storage. All, or some, of the contained cases are stored in a buffer, be it a shuttle system or a Mini Load ASRS. The WES, which orchestrates the activities, determines whether to de-palletize the full pallet or just a select number of layers. If a pallet is partially de-palletized, the remaining layers are sent back to a high bay storage system for later use.

The WES has insight into the orders that are expected to be placed by retail stores in the coming days. Based on that information, it identifies the cases that should be retrieved from bulk storage to fulfill the anticipated demand (first picking phase). The WES also selects a location in the storage buffer to store each case and to determine its orientation. As the orders for the next day are finalized, last-minute adjustments to the staged inventory within the buffer are completed. Buffering systems have multiple levels and aisles and the WES usually stores identical SKUs across many of them.

In the grocery industry, tens of thousands of SKUs are common, with a high percentage of them included in orders every day. Optimally positioning the products in the storage buffer enables them to be retrieved efficiently and in the required sequence. In some systems, cases are stored on trays, which requires automated traying and de-traying technology. Alternatively, cases may be stored directly on the racks. Trays tend to improve the reliability of the system as they can reduce the number of faults generated by defective packaging or product movement. They also introduce additional costs and reduce storage capacity as smaller cases will occupy the same space as larger ones.

The second picking phase (consolidation) and the palletization of orders begins as soon as the storage buffer is sufficiently filled. As the orders for the current day are finalized, pallet configurations are planned. The higher the number of SKUs, the greater the likelihood of congestion and inefficiency, increasing the need for sophisticated retrieval algorithms. Shuttles can efficiently sequence outbound cases using their built-in ability to retrieve multiple cases in parallel. A Mini Load ASRS cannot do this while sustaining sufficient throughput, requiring a downstream sequencer to ensure all cases arrive at the automated palletizer in the right order.

The precise dimensions, weight, and load capacity of each case must be known by the palletization algorithm. Heavier cases must be placed at the bottom, with sufficient load capacity to withstand the weight of cases packed above them. The software must be sophisticated enough to ensure that cases to be unloaded in the same aisle at the retail store are packed near each other on a pallet. Defined rules to avoid placing certain products on the same pallets must also be implemented. An example might be not to pack baby food on the same pallet as hazardous cleaning products. Once calculated, the pallet planning algorithm sends the case retrieval sequence for each pallet to the core WES. The WES responds by issuing directives to the storage buffer to retrieve the designated cases in the required sequence, striving to minimize gaps between cases and maximize loading efficiency at each palletizer. Typically, a dedicated palletizer services each aisle and maximum throughput is achieved by buffering the required cases in that aisle. If several identical cases are to be placed adjacent to one another on the same pallet (to facilitate quick unloading in the store), they are usually stored on different levels in the same aisle within a shuttle system to facilitate parallel retrieval.

As cases begin to arrive back-to-back at a palletizing station, the palletizer loads them onto a pallet one by one, in the location and orientation determined by the pallet building algorithm. Automated palletizers may use articulated arms to place cases on pallets from above. Dematic's Automated Mixed Case Palletizer (AMCAP) and Witron's COM palletizer, both use radial push robots to slide the cases into place, lowering the pallet after each layer is complete. Ergonomic manual palletizing stations may also be used, where workers build the pallets according to the plan determined by the palletizing algorithm. Once a pallet is built, it can be automatically stretch wrapped while the next empty pallet is moved into place.

Packing

After orders have been consolidated, they need to be inspected, packaged, and augmented with manifests and labels in preparation for shipping. Although these services are usually performed manually under the direction of the WES, high volume facilities use specialized automation equipment to reduce the cost per shipment and to improve throughput.

Outbound inspection of goods is done to ensure that the contents of a shipment match its documentation and that no goods are damaged. The automation equipment used is similar to that used for inbound inspection, including hand-held scanners, vision systems, and RFID tunnels.

Scales and dimensional measurement equipment are critical during shipping as the warehouse needs to validate that all transportation constraints that were placed on volume and weight have been respected.

Shipped goods must fit into the enclosure of the truck or container, using only the assigned space for less-than-truckload (LTL) transport and in compliance with legal weight limitations of road vehicles. In automated environments, scales are integrated into the machines that deliver goods to the staging area, be they conveyors, AGVs or AMRs.

Most warehouses package goods into enclosures that are subsequently loaded onto transportation vehicles. Common enclosures that handle discrete goods are poly-mailers or "Jiffy bags," carton boxes, or pallets. Goods need to be secured within the enclosure, and the enclosure must be sealed, properly identified for transportation, and reconciled with a BOL.

Pallet dimensions are standardized by the International Standards Organization (ISO), with the most common size in North America being 48×40 inches. Pallet heights are determined by the height of the products placed on them and the number of stacked layers. They are usually restricted to a maximum of 72 inches, matching the maximum height allowance of trucking companies. To improve the use of space in trucks and containers, pallets are usually defined to be full pallets, using the maximum height allowance, or half pallets which are 36 inches in height. Before pallets are shipped, they are bound by some form of elastic wrapper, often applied by an automated stretch wrap machine. These machines may be stand-alone or integrated with other equipment such as scales and labeling machines. They operate by rotating the pallet in front of a film dispenser that maintains a constant tension of wrapping material.

Carton boxes, as used in parcel shipping, also follow standards although they are more varied than pallets. Box measurements, as opposed to pallet measurements, are fixed in all dimensions. To use boxes for shipping, automated systems need to first select the appropriate box size, based on the dimensions of the goods. This selection process is known as cartonization. For a given set of goods to be shipped, cartonization determines the number of boxes and the specific dimensions required, assigning individual items to specific boxes. Some WMSs and WESs support this functionality natively, and specialty packaging material vendors offer optimized algorithms that integrate with the core system. In most cases, goods will not fit exactly into the dimensions of the shipping box, requiring additional dunnage to be added to the box to avoid damage in transit. There are automated solutions for special cases, but automation of padding material is mostly confined to dispensing the materials for operators to use in filling the cartons.

Carton boxes themselves are procured by warehouses in flat packs, from which individual boxes are separated and formed into their three-dimensional shape. Specialized vendors provide automated case erectors that perform this operation at volume. Box erector machines are configured for a single carton size at a time which reduces their usefulness in retail e-commerce operations that must randomly handle multiple box sizes.

Jiffy bags or poly-mailers are usually filled and sealed manually. Although there are machines available to automate the operation, they tend to be limited to situations where bags have the same, or very similar, contents, as in manufacturing operations. Partially automated machines that assist with the presentation and sealing of the bag exist from multiple manufacturers.

Kitting and Value-Added Services (VAS)

E-commerce warehouses may offer gift wrapping as another potential VAS, often with a choice of wrapping paper as selected by the customer. In this case, the WES displays an image of the selected paper on a monitor. The operator gift wraps the carton and encloses it in a new, slightly larger one.

Special handling may also be offered. If the contained items are fragile, there may be specific packing instructions that must be followed to minimize the likelihood of downstream breakage. The worker will be guided through packaging requirements and the specific materials to use via on-screen instructions.

Modern warehouses frequently perform activities that used to take place in factories, such as finalizing goods for shipping or adding customer or order specific instructions. These light manufacturing tasks are referred to as Kitting in warehouse operations and vary from simple assembly of a group of related items into a single package, to adding optional components to finished products (e.g., adding the correct power supply or plug to electronics equipment according to the destination country of the shipment).

Kitting activities share automation equipment with order consolidation and packaging solutions to ensure the right components are transported to the right workstations at the right time. The operation itself is commonly performed manually under the direction of the WMS or WES as the volume and variability of kitting operations prevent cost-effective use of automation. Automation equipment usually takes the form of pick-and-place robots, aided with some form of vision system.

Once the kit is complete, automation can be used to print and apply the appropriate labels to the packages (e.g., specialized user instructions) and complete the packing and shipping operation.

Manifests and Labels

Packages or pallets shipped from warehouses must be identified to enable reconciliation with the associated documentation. Identification is accomplished by attaching labels containing optical barcodes, QR codes, or RFID tags. For full truck load (FTL) or full container (FCL) load transportation, trailers, and containers are identified in the documentation by associating their ID numbers with the shipment.

Load identifiers are referenced in the shipping manifest or BOL for reconciliation upon receipt at the destination. Labels and documentation can be preattached to the packaging, attached by an operator during shipping via preprinted labels, or custom printed for a specific load. The operator, or an automated scanning sensor, will associate the label with the shipping documents. For direct-to-consumer fulfillment, labels are specific to the carrier that is chosen for delivery (e.g., FedEx, UPS, USPS) and include the name and address of the consumer, as well as any delivery instructions for the operator.

Operations verifying the contents of a package as it is prepared for shipping, creating shipping labels, applying a label to a package, and generating a shipping manifest are frequently performed at the same time. In e-commerce operations, these are high-volume activities. A category of automated machines known as Scan-Label-Apply-Manifest (SLAM), focuses on performing these operations in a single step. These machines were initially custom built by adding sensors and actuators to existing conveyors. They have evolved into standalone machines that are offered by multiple vendors, easily integrated into existing conveyor systems, just before sorting the packages to the shipping docks.

Key Takeaways

- Order consolidation and packing can assume many different forms and are dependent on preceding storage and picking processes and their associated technologies.
- Automated technologies for managing order consolidation of individual items include simple consolidation stations, pouch sorters, Put Walls, and Circular Sorters.
- Mixed-case pallets, commonly used in the grocery industry, are typically sequenced using a two-phase pick process for picking and consolidation.
- Once consolidation is complete, automated inspection machines, cartonization algorithms, case erectors, bag sealers, and value-added service software may be used to semi-automate the inspection and packing process.
- Packages must be labeled for downstream identification to ensure the correct shipping labels are applied.
- Post packing, the application of shipping labels and manifests can be automated and handled in a single step using SLAM machines.

CHAPTER 8

Automated Package and Pallet Sortation

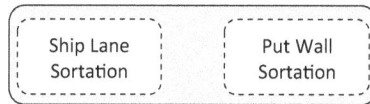

```
┌─────────────────────────────────────────────┐
│  ┌───────────────┐      ┌───────────────┐   │
│  ┆  Ship Lane    ┆      ┆   Put Wall    ┆   │
│  ┆  Sortation    ┆      ┆   Sortation   ┆   │
│  └───────────────┘      └───────────────┘   │
└─────────────────────────────────────────────┘
```

At this stage of the fulfillment process, products were pulled out of storage, picked, consolidated into orders, packed, manifested, and labeled. The next requirement is to sort the finished pallets and packages to their designated shipping lanes. In high-throughput operations, such as e-commerce fulfillment and parcel centers, sortation is an especially critical process. The goal is to transport and divert all packages and pallets to the right place at the right time, which is no easy feat when dealing with upwards of tens of thousands of packages a day.

Package Sortation

The first step in package sortation is to identify the destination shipping lane and the corresponding sorter divert. This is determined by reading the information on the shipping label, if already applied, or from the assigned License Plate Number (LPN). The identifier is captured with an overhead scanner, or scanning tunnel, and sent to the WES. The package weight and dimensions are captured when a package is scanned or retrieved from an earlier inspection, as described in Chapter 7. If any issue is identified (e.g., weight/dimension mismatch, no-read of LPN), the WES issues a command to the sorter controller to divert the package off the line for corrective action. Otherwise, the package is directed to its shipping area and if necessary, to a labeling station. At each stage of the process, a record is written back to the WES database to maintain full visibility of the package's location.

Factors to Consider

A critical decision in the design of a distribution or fulfillment center is the design of the automated sortation system. Throughput requirements, number of sort destinations (diverts), available physical space, package types (e.g., envelopes, cases, and polybags), maximum package weight and dimensions, ease of maintenance, supported temperature range, and overall cost are all factors that must be assessed.

Conveyor-Based Sortation

The most basic form of an automated sortation solution is a modular conveyor system with integrated segments that perform relatively low-speed sortation operations. Examples include Right Angle Transfers, Narrow Belts, and Steerable Wheels. Right Angle Transfers are available in multiple forms, the most common being physical push mechanisms and pneumatic strip belts which rise between the rollers to divert packages. Narrow Belt segments, an example of which is shown in Figure 8.1, offer additional flexibility as belts of varying widths are integrated with rising popup rollers or angled wheels to divert packages diagonally or at 90 degrees. Steerable wheel segments embed small powered rollers with pneumatically controlled actuators to move packages to the left or right. Integrated conveyor diverts can generally sort between 30 and 80 packages per minute, with steerable wheels being at the higher end of that range.

Linear Sorters

A linear sorter resembles a belted conveyor with a built-in takeaway mechanism, diverting items to the right location at the right time. They are often used to sort finished cases or packages rather than individual items, frequently to a shipping dock. Before packages can be sorted, they must be inducted. This is done through an automated merge process, where one or more inbound conveyors connect with the sorter and induct packages in slugs. Prior to induction, a gapper consisting of two conveyor segments operating at slightly different speeds, ensures consistent spacing between cartons. The objective is to minimize spacing

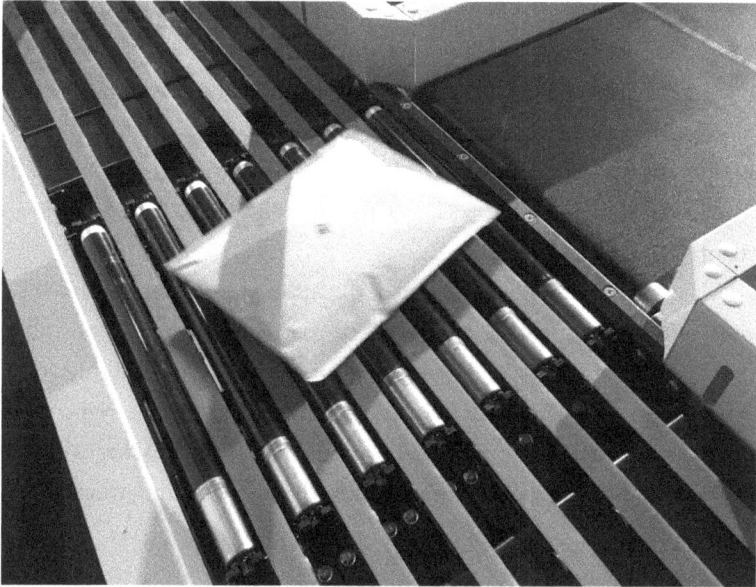

Figure 8.1 Narrow belt sorter from Dematic, with integrated pop-up rollers to divert packages to the left or right. © 2023 by Dematic Corp

while allowing successive diverts to be reached by adjacent packages. Gap optimization is important in order to achieve maximum sorter throughput.

Most linear shoe sorters can move at speeds up to 2 m/s and can sort up to 200 cases per minute, or 12,000 cases per hour. Two driven chains located beside the rails move aluminum slats that have plastic "shoes" mounted on them. When a package reaches its identified divert point, switches controlling the shoes are activated by the controller, triggering them to fire and push the package into its designated chute. The number of shoes that fire for a package varies according to the size of the package.

Linear shoe sorters are a good choice for many shipping applications. Originally designed to handle cases only, many manufacturers have modified their designs to support polybags as well. This is particularly important for e-commerce. Shoe sorters are limited in their ability to handle certain package types, such as small items. They do support relatively high sortation rates while operating at moderate speeds due to their ability to minimize gapping. Limiting the speed also serves to reduce energy consumption and wear and tear. Linear sorters are generally viewed to offer the highest sortation rate per unit of cost and space, which is one reason they are so popular. The diagonal shoe motion also has the ability to divert packages gently. Parallel diverts, including bi-directional diverts, are offered by some manufacturers to further reduce gapping and maximize chute density. Linear sorters can sort small packages that weigh as little as 50 grams to large packages that exceed 50 kg. Figure 8.2 is an example of a shoe sorter from Dematic.

When a shipping label is scanned, the information is sent to the WES to identify the destination chute and to pass it to the sorter controller. The controller monitors the movement of the package according to its slat position and signals the relevant switches to fire at the right time. The off-ramp conveyor leads to the shipping lane, where packages can be offloaded to a holding area or moved directly onto a waiting truck.

Circular (Unit) Sorters

Circular sorters are often used to sort individual items rather than cases. They differ from linear sorters in both design and layout. There are several types of circular sorters, including Bombay, Tilt-tray, Crossbelt, and Push-tray, all sharing similar characteristics. They operate in a large circular loop which often consumes considerable floorspace. This makes them

Figure 8.2 Dematic's FlexSort SL2 sorter, showing the driven chain, the parallel slats, and the mounted shoes. © 2023 by Dematic Corp

less than ideal in smaller, constrained physical environments. They are composed of individual cells, with each cell inducting, moving, and off-loading a single package at a time. Tilt-trays offload packages by tilting the tray along one edge until the product falls out. Bombay sorters open trap doors which force the product to fall out into a chute below. Cross-belts use mini-conveyor belts which run perpendicular to the direction of motion of the sorter. Push trays utilize physical pushers to mechanically divert items into their designated chutes.

An efficient induction process is important to maximize throughput. Unlike linear sorters, no preinduction gapping mechanism is needed as the gapping is built into the structure of the sorter itself. Manual induction may be used though a variety of automated options are available. Angled conveyor-based induction lines that singulate, buffer, orient, synchronize, and transfer awaiting packages onto available cells are common. Robotic alternatives are sometimes used in high-volume environments with limited space. Robots identify and pick individual packages off bulk flow conveyors, placing them onto available cells with sufficient speed to maintain pace with the sorter itself. Vision software and machine learning algorithms are built into the robotic cell to accurately grasp and gently place a wide assortment of items.

Crossbelt sorters are recognized as the fastest, most versatile unit sorters on the market but also the most expensive. They can sort up to 300 packages per minute and support multiple induction points. They are extremely popular in the e-commerce apparel market where products tend not to be fragile. Built with linear induction drives or linear synchronous motors, they operate more quietly than chain-driven sorters. They typically support product weights up to 75 kg and product dimensions up to 1.5 meters in all directions.

Tilt-tray sorters are somewhat less expensive than Crossbelts while offering similar sortation rates. They are, however, more prone to product breakage due to their reliance on gravity. They also tend to be less configurable and are deployed less frequently in modern warehouses. Push-tray sorters are the slowest and least expensive of the circular sortation variants. They are somewhat gentler in their divert operations than Bombay or Tilt-tray sorters. Their sortation rates typically max out around 60 packages per minute. Bombay sorters have fragility limitations similar to Tilt trays and as such are used more regularly in apparel, fashion, and pharmaceutical industries. Their throughput can reach approximately 200 cases per minute with a lower price point than Crossbelts. They also utilize less floor space than other circular sorters as their chutes are located below the surface, making them more attractive in space-limited environments.

Prior to induction, shipping labels of packages are scanned so the WES can identify the designated divert chutes and send them to the sorter controller. Packages may be inducted at one or multiple induction stations. As the associated sorter cell approaches its target chute, the controller activates the cell to tilt the tray, move the conveyor, open the trap door, or slide the pusher. When a chute is full, its contents are moved to a shipping area before it accepts additional packages. Inducted packages destined for that chute will continue to circulate on their cells until it is ready to receive new packages.

Modular Plastic Belted Sorters

Modular plastic belted (MPB) sorters can achieve high sortation rates in constrained spaces and have a number of unique characteristics. They utilize free-spinning rollers that are selectively and directionally activated. Space requirements are often lower than with alternative sorters as no external safety guarding is required. They are extremely flexible and can handle a wide array of package types including envelopes, totes, polybags, cases, books, and heavy pallets. MPB sorters can sort packages ranging from about 5 centimeters to 1.5 meters in length and can do so in bulk, without the need for prior singulation. They can also handle awkwardly shaped items like rubber tires, which are often unsortable with other technologies.

By deploying a small section of MPB sortation equipment, the layout of a facility may change significantly. MPBs are able to bi-directionally sort up to 12,000 cases per hour while simultaneously changing their orientation and alignment. The speed of each package may be manipulated on the fly, minimizing gapping, and maximizing efficiency. On the downside, these sorters can be quite expensive and often operate in limited temperature zones. They also offer somewhat lower sortation rates than many linear or circular alternatives. Intralox is a leading provider in this market with their ARB technology.

The position of each package on an MPB sorter is tracked by the conveyor controller through the combination of belt positioning and software algorithms. Application Programming Interfaces (APIs) are externalized to the WES, enabling it to direct the sorter to move, rotate, align, and divert packages individually or in slugs. The sorter controller executes its directed tasks and provides status information back to the WES upon completion or failure.

AMRs

Figure 8.3 shows Tompkins Robotics t-Sort solution which manages sortation using a fleet of dedicated AMRs. As with traditional sorters, items may be manually or automatically inducted. With automated induction, a mini-conveyor segment is attached to the top of the AMR which butts up against an inbound conveyor. In the case of manual induction, packages are placed directly onto the AMR sortation platform. Regardless of the induction approach, each package is scanned in order to couple it with the AMR. This enables the WES to send destination instructions to the controller software managing the fleet. When an AMR receives its mission, it moves autonomously to the designated location. Upon arrival, its mini-conveyor segment or tilt tray is triggered to unload the package. The fleet controller signals the completion of the task to the WCS which then dispatches the AMR to retrieve a new package.

There are advantages and disadvantages to using AMRs for sorting. On the positive front, the solutions are relatively quick to implement and utilize less floor space than a "bolted to the ground" sorter. The routes to a target chute are more direct, there is no single point of failure, they

Figure 8.3 Tompkins Robotics' t-Sort sortation solution using a swarm of Tilt-tray enabled AMRs. © 2023 by Tompkins Robotics

scale well, and they enable low-volume sortation to be managed with just a handful of bots. As volume grows, it is simple to add more AMRs into the fleet to linearly increase capacity. The speed of the AMRs is between 2 m/s and 3 m/s, similar to the speed of most sorters. It is easy to add new destinations and they can be located anywhere in the designated sortation area. Both capital costs and ongoing operating costs may be lower than with traditional sorters, largely because there is less unused capacity.

Despite the advantages, in high-volume environments, it is often difficult for AMR-based sortation to achieve the same throughput levels as linear or circular sorters. This is due to the increased spacing between packages. Additionally, when a large number of AMRs are deployed in a condensed area, congestion may occur, slowing down movement.

The integration of a WES with AMR-based sortation management is relatively straightforward. Packages are scanned when inducted and the data is passed back to the WES by the scanner, which then transmits the destination identifier to the fleet's sortation manager, which takes care of the rest. It assigns the task to an available AMR and informs the WES when the job is done. From the perspective of the WES, the interface is similar to that of a traditional conveyor. This makes hybrid sortation relatively easy to manage. Some items may be more appropriately sorted with AMRs and others with traditional sorters. In certain environments, AMRs are deployed in order to augment capacity during peak periods.

Summary of Options

The automated package sortation options can be summarized as shown in Table 8.1.

Table 8.1 Summary of case transport options

TYPE	Price	Throughput	Install time	Scalability	Package variability
Conveyor based	Low	Low	Low	Low	Med-High
Linear	Med	Med-High	High	Low	Low
Circular	Med-High	High	High	Low	Med
Modular Plastic	High	Med	Med	Low-Med	Med-High
AMR	Low-Med	Low-Med	Low-Med	High	Med

Pallet Sortation

Pallet sortation is less complicated than package sortation for two reasons: (1) There is less variation between pallets as the contents stored on each are of little importance. (2) The number of pallets being sorted is at least an order of magnitude less than the number of packages. Due to the relatively low speeds and the moderate throughput requirements, there is little difference between pallet conveyance and sortation. Outbound pallet sortation is used in distribution centers when cases are palletized before they are shipped. Grocery and Food and Beverage are two such verticals. Despite the relative simplicity, there are higher costs, higher throughput, and more flexible options, as well as ones that perform better in harsh environments.

Factors to Consider

To determine the most effective way to sort ready pallets, the factors that must be considered are: maximum weight capacity, throughput, floorspace, temperature, cleanliness, moisture levels, and quality of flooring. Pallet conveyors, monorails, and AGVs (or AMRs) are the primary options. In some environments, a combination may yield the best solution.

Pallet Conveyors

There are a variety of pallet conveyor designs, including Drag Chain, Chain Driven Live Roller (CDLR), Belt Driven Live Roller (BDLR), and 24V DC powered. Popup-rollers or turntables are used to divert the pallets by turning them 90 degrees toward the shipping lanes. The conveyors move at a relatively slow speed, typically between 10 and 20 meters per minute.

Drag Chain pallet conveyors utilize parallel strands of roller chain without belts or rollers. They are often used to transport and sort specialized pallets with formed feet which prevents them from being inducted onto other types of conveyors. They also support very heavy pallet loads, up to 2,500 kg.

CDLR conveyors utilize chains to drive their rollers. Inducted pallets must be well-formed and have flat bottoms. These conveyors are easy to configure, are available in a variety of widths, support configurable curves, and the spacing between rollers is customizable. They work well in rugged environments, including those containing significant debris, oil, or moisture.

BDLR conveyors work best when transporting relatively light pallet loads. A single drive controls a long belt that moves on pressure rollers. Carrier rollers are mounted above the belt to transport the pallets. The price tends to be lower than CDLR conveyors but so are the weight capacity and the speed.

24V DC-powered conveyors are a good option for transporting lighter pallet loads. They are more expensive than BDLR conveyors but are quick to install, easy to maintain, and support pallet accumulation effectively. A series of defined zones, each consisting of approximately 10 rollers, are independently controlled. The drive roller in each zone has an embedded 24V motor which is connected to a dedicated drive. All zone drives communicate status and sensor information amongst themselves, enabling support of contactless accumulation.

Monorails

While more expensive than pallet conveyors, monorails offer a number of advantages. They can be aerial mounted on aluminum rails that are suspended from the ceiling, or floor mounted on electric rails. Aerial-mounted solutions may be chosen when a warehouse floor is not level. Both versions can move up to 10 times faster than most pallet conveyors, traveling up to 200 meters per minute. They also require less time for pallet drop-off and pickup. They are particularly efficient when transporting pallets long distances and are easily designed to wind through a building or to weave in and out of various stations. When throughput requirements are low, a subset of the trolleys may be removed from the circuit and parked to reduce power consumption. A dedicated controller manages the overall movement to avoid bottlenecks, load and unload the trolleys, and manage power consumption.

Supported pallet load weights are similar to CDLR conveyors, typically in the 1,500 kg range.

AGVs and AMRs

To maximize flexibility, AGVs and AMRs may be the best pallet transport and sortation solutions for a warehouse. They can transport pallets directly from storage rack units to trucks, without the need to drop them off at intermediate locations. Some are autonomous forklift trucks, able to lift pallets in and out of rack locations. Others, like the one shown in Figure 8.4, are flatbed vehicles with attachments that enable induction, transport, and offloading. AGVs require offboard elements or equipment (e.g., magnetic guide tape, wire paths, laser reflective tape) to localize themselves. AMRs require no such infrastructure, as they are equipped with Simultaneous Localization and Mapping (SLAM) technology, enabling them to learn new environments using vehicle-mounted LiDAR equipment and cameras. AMRs can weave their way around workers while AGVs move on predetermined paths, stopping when obstructed until their path is cleared.

AMRs and AGVs are particularly effective for sortation when throughput needs are lower and dedicated floorspace is unavailable. They are not a good choice in dirty or harsh environments. They operate safely alongside human workers and are particularly cost-effective when transport routes are long. Larger AMRs and AGVs can support pallets up to 2,000 kg in weight with maximum speeds of about 2 m/s. Some larger pallet truck AMRs can move even heavier loads, while tow-tractor AMRs are designed to move multiple connected loads at once, up to a total weight of about 4,500 kg.

The individual cost of AMRs and AGVs varies based on capability, weight capacity, lift mechanisms, and speed, but they are often an excellent option for transportation and sortation in low-volume environments. They tend to range between $50K and $200K. When they are not performing sortation tasks, they can be used to execute other warehouse functions such as receiving, put-away, or staging.

Figure 8.4 Pallet transportation and sortation performed using an OTTO 1500 from OTTO Motors, a division of Clearpath Robotics. © 2023 by Clearpath Robotics

Summary of Options

The automated pallet sortation options can be summarized as shown in Table 8.2.

Table 8.2 Pallet sortation options

TYPE	Price	Throughput	Install time	Scalability	Weight capacity	Flexibility
Pallet Conveyors	Low-Med	Med-High	Med-High	Low	Med-High	Low
Monorail	Med-High	High	Med-High	Med	Med	Med
AGV or AMR	Med-High	Low	Low	High	Med-High	High

Key Takeaways

- Automated sortation equipment is often among the most impactful investments made in a warehouse. The return on investment can be rapid and significant.
- Throughput needs to be modeled and future growth understood before a sortation design is finalized.

- Automated package sortation may be achieved using conveyors, linear sorters, circular sorters, modular plastic sorters, or AMRs, each with various advantages and disadvantages.
- Automated package sortation may use pallet conveyors, monorails, AGVs, or AMRs.

CHAPTER 9

Staging and Truck Loading

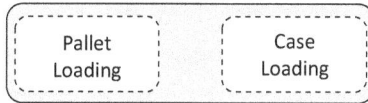

Observing the action inside modern automated warehouses gives the impression of a well-choreographed flow of goods from receiving to storage and from storage to shipping, with no interruptions or bottlenecks. This continuous flow is interrupted when goods are shipped out of the warehouse. Shipping relies on transportation vehicles with finite capacity operating on discrete trip schedules. Even with the best scheduling, shipping introduces "fulfillment batches" that correspond to each departing transport truck.

Warehouses use staging areas to accumulate and organize the goods that are to be shipped out on the same truck. From these staging areas, goods are loaded and secured into transportation enclosures (e.g., shipping containers) or directly into the vehicle.

Shipping units may be parcels, packages, pallets, or whole containers. They determine the core processes and technologies used for staging and loading, with other factors such as the type of transportation routing (e.g., point-to-point or distribution), regulatory considerations (e.g., import/export), and the nature of the goods (e.g., refrigerated, hazardous) also playing a role.

Container loading refers to the actual movement of a container onto a transportation chassis. This type of operation primarily takes place in ocean terminals and rail yards, using specialized cranes, forklift trucks, or AGVs and is not the focus of this book.

Pallet Loading

Pallets are delivered to staging areas using appropriate transportation and sorting mechanisms as discussed in Chapter 8. They are stored directly on the floor or stacked according to weight, strength, and fragility when floor space is at a premium. From their staging locations, pallets are moved into the truck in sequence. The loading sequence is designed to facilitate the expected unloading process at the receiving facility, which is particularly important in the case of Less-than-Truckload (LTL) transportation, where a single truck is expected to unload its contents through a series of stops. The sequence in which pallets are loaded is determined by the WMS or WES in collaboration with the TMS, often using specialized software modules.

The sequence and packaging produced by the software must respect the maximum volume, weight, and weight balance tolerances of the vehicle and its enclosure. The order and position of the pallets in the enclosure must also take into account the stackability and stability of the pallets themselves, with heavier pallets positioned nearer to the bottom to improve the stability of the load and to avoid damaging any goods.

Manual loading of pallets is done using manual or powered pallet jacks when at floor level and using warehouse forklift trucks when stacking multiple levels inside an enclosure. By replicating manual movements, autonomous pallet carriers or forklifts can be used for automated truck loading.

In contrast with equipment used to transport pallets within the warehouse, equipment for truck loading cannot fully rely on pre-positioned guides or markers. Instead, it incorporates environmental sensors like vision and radar to detect the environment, coupled with sophisticated navigation and planning software to avoid obstacles and to identify the precise location for each pallet.

An alternative is to use automated loading platforms. These specialized platforms, which were also discussed in Chapter 4 as part of the receiving process, may require modifications to truck floors. These dedicated machines utilize a conveyor platform mounted on a set of tractor wheels, enabling them to move pallets in and out of the truck as necessary. Rollers or belts move the pallets along the platform and a lift or hoist is used to raise and lower the pallets into the truck as they reach the end of the platform. The platform may be long enough to double as a staging area for pallets to be loaded, creating a slug for insertion into the truck in a single shot.

Parcel Loading

Loading processes for loose parcels are different when designed for transportation between distribution centers versus between a fulfillment center and a final destination.

Parcel Loading for Transport Between Distribution Centers

When moved between distribution centers, packages are usually loaded into full trailers. This loading process has very different requirements than pallet loading. The priorities are efficiency in volumetric density and speed of loading and unloading. Volume, weight, and balance constraints need to be respected but they are much less sensitive to the presence or position of any single package. Goods are usually enclosed in protective material, either a carton box or a padded envelope, to reduce the risk of damage. Sequencing of packages is not important for the load itself as the whole trailer will be emptied at the destination.

The main challenge is to maximize the fill of the trailer and to do it quickly, free up the dock, and minimize the idle time of the trucks. Boom and articulated conveyors are commonly used to automate the delivery of packages to human loaders stationed in a truck. These conveyors are not rigidly attached to the floor or to other fixed points in the warehouse. Their supports can move and they can adjust their length and joint angles to adapt to varying start and end points. When used for truck loading, their origin is connected to the staging area or to the output of the shipping sorter. The end of the conveyor telescopes into the trailer. As the trailer is filled, the conveyor retracts, always remaining adjacent to the "face" of the load until the trailer is full.

Loading of loose packages is a labor-intensive activity due to the variability of the packages and the vehicles, and the challenge of installing traditional automation equipment into constrained spaces.

New technologies enable flexible automation solutions by mounting equipment on mobile platforms. Automation vendors are now offering a variety of robotic solutions for vehicle loading. One approach is to use an articulated arm mounted onto the end of an extension boom. The robot picks packages delivered by a loading conveyor that is extended into the cargo bay of the truck, depositing them into their designated locations. Articulated robots use multipoint vacuum grippers to control the package orientation while providing enough suction to handle the weight of individual packages. An alternative robot configuration consists of a small conveyor that connects the end of the feeding conveyor to a platform that slides the packages into their preordained positions. These applications have not gained commercial acceptance yet, largely due to their relatively high cost per unit of throughput.

In either case, accurately positioning the actuator is prescribed by software that preplans the packages in the load. When packages are uniform, this approach is relatively reliable and fast. For loads with uneven package sizes or irregular layouts, position planning needs to be guided by sensor data that outlines the actual "shape" of the load in real time to ensure that the new package is placed in the right location. This results in more software complexity and yields a slower and less reliable solution.

Parcel Loading for Distribution to Multiple Drop Locations

There are two major differences when loading packages for distribution to multiple drop locations. The first is that the target vehicle is an urban delivery van rather than a highway trailer. The second is the need to prioritize the cost of the delivery run, sacrificing volumetric efficiency and loading speed to minimize delivery times. Packages must be staged and loaded so that retrieval along the route does not require any reshuffling by the driver. They may be pre-positioned in containers by sections of road, or the delivery van itself may have internal racks to help organize the packages. Commercially available automated loading solutions for these environments don't yet exist. Some material handling manufacturers, in collaboration with delivery companies and vehicle manufacturers, have prototyped systems that integrate staging and vehicle loading. These solutions preload standard racks in the staging area after which they are inserted into the vehicle. Empty racks from returning vehicles are removed and replaced with preloaded ones. The challenges facing these solutions are their relatively high cost and low load densities.

Key Takeaways

- Staging and truck loading processes are relatively difficult to automate because of the high variability in the equipment and the environment, compared to processes that are internal to a warehouse.
- Pallet loading is automated using conveyor-based solutions or autonomous forklift vehicles.
- Automation technology for carton loading is less mature than pallet loading due to the complexity of the packing algorithms and the precision of the actuators required to reliably position cartons in confined spaces.

CHAPTER 10

What About Returns?

The growth of e-commerce created an unintended, negative side-effect: the explosive rise in the number of returns that many retailers must manage. In some industries, companies are dealing with return rates that exceed 40 percent. What's worse, in the case of lower-value goods, the processing cost of each return often exceeds the value of the goods themselves. Automation technologies have been developed to address many of these challenges, minimize the associated costs, and return the received inventory to a state that makes them available for resale as soon as possible.

Why Such High Return Rates?

According to a Walker Sands report, 54 percent of e-commerce purchasers say that free returns or exchanges factor heavily in their buying decisions. Said differently: without generous return policies, online retailers are likely to face a significant decline in demand. The most common reasons for returns include incorrect size or color, gift return, damaged item, wrong product, and incorrect product description. In some sectors, such as apparel, consumers often buy several items with the intent to return all of them, or all but one. It's an easy way to see what fits or looks good and to simulate an in-store purchase experience. Unfortunately, it's very costly for retailers.

According to the National Retail Federation (NRF), the merchandise return rate across all sectors and channels exceeded 16 percent in 2022. E-commerce return rates are two to three times higher in some of them, due in part to the near-painless consumer experience offered by many large online retailers. These numbers tend to be the highest in apparel and some high-dollar-value industries like electronics. Retailers understand that despite the costs, a positive return experience influences future buying decisions. Additionally, a wealth of useful information is accessible to retailers if they analyze the reasons behind the returns. Investing in cost-effective, automated returns solutions is becoming increasingly common in many distribution and fulfillment centers.

Some retailers elect to outsource their returns processing to third parties who manage it on their behalf, others set up dedicated returns facilities, and some incorporate returns processing into their core fulfillment centers.

The Generic Returns Process

Before we explore the various automation options that can help streamline the process, it is important to understand the five steps involved in most online returns:

- Preparation: A Return Merchandise Authorization (RMA) and a shipping label are printed by the consumer or included in the original package. The RMA slip, which is a pre-authorization for the return, is inserted into the returned package and the shipping label is affixed to its outside. If the product is ineligible for return, an RMA label is not made available to the customer.
- Validation: Upon arrival at the returns site, the RMA is scanned to identify the corresponding order and to check that all preconditions are met. If they have been, the contents of the package are examined to validate that the item was returned in full and to assess its condition.
- Disposition and Repair: Based on a physical inspection of the item and a review of its value, a decision is made whether or not to grant a refund and to assign a disposition. Potential dispositions are to return the product to inventory, send it out for repair, send it for testing and repackaging, or declare it as scrap.
- Action: If a refund is approved, the ERP system is updated to process the corresponding financial transactions. If it is declined, the decision and the reason are communicated back

to the customer, with a reference number and additional
customer service contact information.

- Resale: When an item is deemed ready for resale, potentially
after being repaired, repackaged, or recoded as an open-box
item, the WMS is updated and the item is reinducted into
inventory.

Automated Returns Approaches

Due to complexity in determining the correct disposition of a returned
item and the frequent need to perform services before it is ready for resale,
not all steps in a returns process are automatable. Many can be stream-
lined, however, and we analyze these opportunities by phase.

Preparation

Why do most of us like to shop at Amazon? Two of the reasons are the
vast array of products available on their platform and their free and fast
delivery. Another is their easy returns and rapid refunds. Amazon has
figured out how to make the returns process more convenient than it is at
brick-and-mortar stores. As consumers, we simply sign into our accounts,
select the item to be returned, choose a reason code, and print off the
RMA and shipping labels. We drop the package off at a depot around the
corner and usually, by the end of the day, we are notified that our refund
has been processed. It's smooth and efficient, and it makes us want to buy
from them over and over again.

While the return is made easy for the consumer, it is not nearly as
easy for the retailer. Most of the complexity lies in the software. An
online portal must be developed for customers to view and select their
prior purchases, submit the required information, and print out the
return-related forms. A reference to the submitted information is linked
to the original order in the retailer's backend system, and validated for
accuracy when the returned items are received. Some retailers don't make
it this easy for their customers, which serves to lessen their return rates
but a single bad experience may also harm their reputation and impact
future purchasing decisions.

Validation

Returned items are typically received at return or fulfillment centers as individual cases. The first step in streamlining the returns process is to manage the queue of inbound items efficiently. This is often done using automated conveyors that move items to staffed validation stations. Assigned workers will open the packages and scan the barcodes of the inserted RMA forms, displaying the original order data on an adjacent monitor. If no RMA form was enclosed or if no match was found, the item will be conveyed to an "unidentified returns" station where a decision is made regarding the next steps. Otherwise, the worker will initiate the disposition phase, or if greater expertise is required (e.g., if a high-value electronic item is being returned), dispatch the item to a specialized returns station.

Disposition and Repair

Various automation technologies are available to at least partially streamline dispositions. While not perfect, they do simplify the process. Unit Sorters may be used to increase efficiency, particularly when there are large numbers of complex products being returned, all requiring specialized disposition stations. They are used to create a high-speed routing mechanism, moving items to the correct station and, if required, to specialized repair stations.

Consider a retailer who sells pricy, motorized toy cars that require home assembly, together with a wide range of other products. If a car is returned with the reason code "product malfunction," it is likely being returned without the original packaging intact. Retailers have the right to refuse a refund if associated parts are missing. Even if the returned item is sent to a specialized disposition station, the worker may not be able to easily detect if all the parts were returned. By emptying the contents of the box into a tote, and using an overhead vision system to identify the contained components, the disposition process can be simplified. All expected parts are shown on an overhead monitor while the scanned parts are detected by the vision system and displayed alongside them. If missing items or discrepancies are detected, it is easy for a worker to assign the correct disposition and update the customer record. The technology is especially useful when high-value items are being processed.

Based on its disposition, the software will receive the item into inventory and determine where to route it next, be it to a repair station, a repackaging station, an induction station, a customer service station, or to scrap. The routing may utilize conveyors, unit sorters, or AMRs.

Action

According to joint research conducted by the NRF and Appriss Research, approximately 10.3 percent of all returns are fraudulent. In an attempt to mitigate the problem, some companies are turning to AI to develop more customized decision processes. Not only is it used to help identify product issues, but it can also be used to identify customer patterns. Those with a history of fraudulent returns may not be granted the same rights as loyal, repeat customers.

In many cases, determining whether or not to offer a full refund is clear and it is granted by the same person who assigns the disposition. In other cases, particularly when the value of the product is high, the decision may not be obvious. In those cases, the returns software, usually a subcomponent of the WMS, queues the order and the associated returns disposition information for a customer service representative to make a decision. The representative also creates an incident number and contacts the customer via email to provide additional instructions and options.

When a decision is made, be it to offer a full refund, a partial refund, or no refund, the WMS updates the ERP system to initiate the associated financial transactions.

Resale

The ideal outcome of returns processing is to make the item available for resale as quickly as possible. Products that are repaired and repackaged and those that were returned unopened may be sent to inventory as fully warrantied open-box items or as new items. Those designated as open-box items are assigned a new SKU, enabling them to be inventoried and sold as unique items. Those that were returned unopened retain their original SKUs.

Pouch sorters, as described in Chapter 7, are particularly effective in managing returns. After an item is validated to be in saleable condition, it can be scanned and inducted into a pouch, either manually or using an automated induction station. The content of the pouch is updated in the WMS, after which it becomes immediately available for resale. Overhead pouches with saleable items can reside anywhere in the warehouse, so there is no need to convey the returned item to a specific location. Due to stringent weight and size limitations, pouch systems cannot be used for any type of product. They are effective for smaller, lighter items, making them particularly popular in the apparel industry. Pouch systems may be deployed to manage regular and reverse logistics simultaneously, or smaller systems may be deployed strictly for returns. If used for returns only, those items would typically be retrieved to fulfill orders first.

AMRs and conveyors can also be used to automate the return of an item. In the case of shelf-to-person operations, a shelf-carrying robot is dispatched to the returns station and the item is inducted into a designated bin. The AMR then drops the shelf at a new, randomly selected location. The inventory in the bin and the location of the shelf are updated in the WMS.

Conveyors may be used to streamline returns when storing items in more conventional locations like static shelving or an ASRS. In some cases, the process is completed by scanning the returned item and dropping it directly onto a conveyor. The WMS or WES will select a storage location and send the required commands to the conveyor and ASRS controllers.

The key analysis to be done by retailers is the amount of money to spend on returns processing, versus the value they are getting out of it. What makes it complicated is that only some of the value is associated with reselling the item. In many cases, more value is realized by understanding the reason for the return. Data can be analyzed to help determine what, if any, changes should be made to the product or if it should be discontinued altogether. For some products, particularly those with low value and low return rates, it may make sense to dispose of the goods immediately or to grant the consumer a refund without requiring their return.

Key Takeaways

- In some industries, return rates are as high as 40 percent. The manner in which retailers handle returns can have a dramatic impact on their success. Automating the process is becoming increasingly important.
- An investment in returns automation should be assessed against the percentage of items returned, the level of fraud, the average value of products sold, and the customer loyalty to be gained by streamlining the process.
- Intelligent, web-based software may significantly improve the returns experience for consumers, and simplify it for retailers.
- Items must be quality checked to assess if they are resalable. If they are, the objective is to store returned items for reassignment to orders as quickly as possible.
- A number of automation technologies can be used to streamline the returns process. They include intelligent software algorithms, overhead scanners, integrated scales, pouch sorters, AMRs, ASRSs, and conveyors.

CHAPTER 11

Automation Using AGVs and AMRs

We have referenced AGVs and AMRs throughout this book. Due to their increasing relevance to the industry and the impact they will have on the design of next-generation automated warehouses, a chapter dedicated to their operation is warranted.

AGV Usage in Warehouses

The first AGV, a tow truck following the path of a wire embedded in the floor of its facility, was deployed by Barrett Electronics in the 1950s. Since then, their use has expanded to include tasks that were previously only achievable with forklift trucks, conveyors, or manual carts. Their operation tends to be repetitive and is focused on the transport of pallet loads of goods from one location to another. In warehouses, they are often used to move inventory from long-term storage locations to forward-pick locations, from packing areas to shipping docks, for cross-docking operations, and to automate the trailer-loading or unloading processes. As shown in Figure 11.1, multiple AGV variants have emerged over the years:

- Automated Guided Carts (AGCs) travel low to the ground and usually have flatbed tops. They automate the movement of cases, totes, racks, or pallets, from one location to another.
- Forklift AGVs are equipped with pallet-handling forks. They come in many shapes, sizes, load capacities, lift heights, turning radiuses, and swing capabilities. Reach trucks typically lift loads to heights ranging between 5 and 15 meters. Some are able to operate in very narrow aisles and reach levels that rival those of Unit Load ASRSs. Some

Figure 11.1 A Forklift AGV is shown on the left, and a tugger AGV is shown on the right, both offered by Dematic. © 2023 by Dematic Corp

vendors manufacture hybrid vehicles, capable of operating in either driver or driverless mode. Most of these vehicles are built using automation kits that integrate with existing electrical and mechanical components of standard forklift truck lines.

- Tugger AGVs pull one or more nonpowered, load-carrying vehicles behind them in a train formation. They usually travel long distances in warehouses, with multiple drop-off and pick-up locations along their route.

AGV Navigation

Over the years, technology options for guiding AGVs along their routes have increased—from inductive wires to magnetic tapes, tags, lasers, and camera-based vision systems.

With wire-based navigation, radio frequency signals are transmitted to sensors affixed to the underside of the AGV from a wire embedded in the floor. Magnetic tape-based systems are similar but offer additional flexibility as the tape is removable and can be repositioned to alter the guide path, sacrificing durability for flexibility. Tag-based systems guide vehicles using Quick Response (QR) codes, RFID tags, or magnetic dots. The vehicles are equipped with sensors that follow the route laid out by the markers. Laser-based systems use reflective tape that is affixed to fixed locations in a warehouse, usually on walls or poles. Transmitters and receivers on the AGVs measure the distance and angle to these locations, enabling the AGV position to be repeatedly calculated through triangulation. With camera-based vision systems, no infrastructure modifications are required. Instead, an operator drives a vehicle along a desired path while an onboard camera captures a continuous stream of images to build a 3D map and to record the drive path within it. When a route changes, the driver simply repeats the process to learn the new route. Adequate lighting conditions and high-quality cameras are required to capture sufficiently high-resolution images.

The advantages and disadvantages of the various AGV navigation approaches are summarized in Table 11.1.

Table 11.1 *Advantages and disadvantages of the most common AGV navigation technologies*

	Inductive wire	Magnetic tape	Floor tags	Laser guided	Vision
Accuracy	Excellent	Good	Fair	Excellent	Fair
Installation Cost	High	Medium	Medium	Low	Medium
Vehicle cost	Low-Medium	Low	Low-Medium	High	High
Reliability	Good	Good	Good	Excellent	Fair
Flexibility	Poor	Fair	Fair	Fair	Good
Installation Time	High	Low	Low	Low	Low
Maintenance	Medium-High	High	Low	Low-Medium	Low

AGV Control

A dedicated software system with select components running on the vehicle and others on an offboard server controls the movement and actions of an AGV fleet. Depending on the design, controllers onboard the vehicles may be given considerable control over their own movement as well as the ability to communicate with each other. Alternatively, they may be granted very little control, relying on offboard software to send streams of low-level commands. Onboard solutions use more sophisticated sensors and complex internal software, enabling them to assign tasks amongst themselves and to respond independently to changing real-time conditions. Offboard software, if it exists, acts as a fleet's mission control system—managing all tasks, determining routes, and directing traffic. In this case, onboard software is usually relatively simple, responsible only for executing missions as they are received.

AGVs are typically controlled by zones to minimize congestion and the risk of collisions. A central server issues commands to a wireless transmitter on regular intervals. With each command, the transmitter emits a signal to a zone. Vehicles are equipped with sensors that transmit responses after detecting a signal. If an AGV is already in a zone, a STOP signal is sent to prevent other AGVs from entering until a subsequent CLEAR signal is transmitted.

For added safety, collisions can be avoided by equipping AGVs with sonic or optical sensors. They transmit signals and measure the associated responses to detect objects or people that may be in their way. Bumper sensors are usually added for additional safety, abruptly stopping the vehicle if contact is made with an undetected object. In many implementations, zone-based control and collision control are used simultaneously. Zone-based control serves as the primary traffic control mechanism and collision detection and bumper control are used as fail-safe mechanisms.

AGVs, unlike AMRs, do not have the ability to navigate off a predetermined path. If an object gets in their way, their only option is to come to an immediate stop until it is cleared. Vehicles may be controlled individually or as a fleet. The size of the fleet is usually small, typically less than 15 to 20 vehicles.

AGV Pros and Cons

AGVs offer a number of advantages over traditional "bolted-down" automation technologies like conveyors and sorters. Foremost among them is that they safely share their space with human workers. With onboard proximity and collision detection sensors, they also improve workplace safety conditions in a warehouse. They reliably automate predictable and repetitive tasks and can eliminate unnecessary walking or physically demanding activities. While AGVs are costly, with prices typically ranging between \$40K and \$200K, they are able to operate 24 hours a day and offer lower cost fluctuations than human labor performing similar tasks. They are also portable and scalable. A fleet can easily be moved to a new building and new units can be added with minimal effort as business demands grow. They are also much more flexible than convey/sort solutions, able to manage material flow from a wide array of source points to a large number of reconfigurable endpoints.

AGVs have a number of disadvantages as well. Depending on the environment, their cost may be high when measured against raw throughput. In high-volume environments, it may be difficult to achieve the same storage and retrieval rates as ASRS machines, or the same transport rates as conveyors. Since they are unable to dynamically alter their paths, overall throughput may be reduced because of congestion and multiple stops and starts. To maximize the value of an AGV investment, it is usually necessary to run a multiple-shift operation, making it easier to justify the capital costs against the labor costs of manual forklift truck drivers.

The Arrival of AMRs

The first commercially available AMR, named HelpMate, was released in the 1990s. Developed by HelpMate Robotics, it navigated autonomously through hospital hallways to deliver meals and other supplies without using wires, tape, or other markers. In the 2000s, AMRs surfaced in home applications, primarily as vacuuming robots popularized by iRobot's Roomba. In the 2010s, AMR technology began to find its way into warehouses.

AMRs differ from AGVs in that no infrastructure changes are required for them to operate. They often move lighter loads, including totes and cases, though that distinction is unrelated to their definition. Most AMR vendors offer a range of vehicle types, with either case-load, pallet-load, or shelf-load capacities. They navigate freely in their environment using sensors to pinpoint their location on digital maps constructed during a setup phase. This enables them to dynamically change their preferred path to a destination and to circumvent any obstacles that unexpectedly get in their way.

During setup, onboard LiDAR systems pulse high-frequency laser beams at fixed objects such as walls and racks. Integrated imaging sensors capture the reflected light from the objects to measure their respective distances. The collected data is processed into a point cloud (a large dataset of 3D points in space) and fused together with associated camera images. Map generation software, running on powerful backend servers, converts the data into a digital map which is then downloaded onto all AMRs in the fleet.

Using SLAM, each AMR is able to determine where it is at all times. Software algorithms merge data from onboard camera sensors, LiDARs, and other sources like vehicle wheel odometry, to pinpoint its precise location on the pregenerated map. The software implementing these algorithms is very sophisticated. Complex calculations must be executed several times per second, running on low-power, low-memory embedded microprocessors.

Most AMR vendors offer proprietary map generation technologies. Those who are able to generate the highest quality maps in the shortest period of time can claim a competitive advantage. This is especially important because map generation is not a one-time operation. Each time the layout of a facility changes, the corresponding map must be modified. Mapping logic is also invoked when unexpected, semipermanent obstacles are encountered by vehicles in the fleet (e.g., an aisle may be closed for maintenance). An effective, on-demand remapping strategy improves the performance of the fleet by avoiding obstacles, without requiring individual vehicles to figure out the alternatives each time.

Comparing AGVs and AMRs

AMRs are clever enough to move around obstacles while AGVs are not. They are usually equipped with LiDAR sensors, 3D depth cameras, and a variety of additional sensors to facilitate the identification of surrounding static or dynamic obstacles.

A common misconception is that AMRs differ from AGVs by their form factor, with AGVs being large fork-based, pallet-carrying vehicles and AMRs being smaller, flat-top, lighter-load carrying vehicles. In reality, their distinction is related to the differences in their localization, path generation, and obstacle avoidance technologies.

AMR Swarm Control

Perhaps the most compelling feature of AMRs is their ability to function in large, centrally controlled swarms. Unlike traditional automation solutions which necessitate the integration of a wide range of equipment, each with a unique controller, all AMRs in a fleet from the same manufacturer are fundamentally the same. They may have different attachments that enable them to perform unique tasks, and they may come in varying shapes, sizes, and load capacities, but they all move around, receive commands, and communicate the same way.

Because the AMRs in today's fleets tend to be standardized, they are relatively simple and quick to install. In many cases, services offered by the AMR vendor or integrator are not required when commissioning or decommissioning robots. This is particularly helpful for businesses with seasonal demand variations as it enables them to easily lease additional robot capacity as required. Fleets may be large, often in the hundreds of units, with each robot assigned one task at a time, typically by a centralized orchestration engine. The engine may reside on a local server or it may be deployed as a cloud service, making it relatively easy for vendors to offer pay-as-you-go, Robot-as-a-Service (RaaS) subscription options.

A recent technology trend gaining considerable attention is the multi-agent orchestration platform. The technology is based on the premise that heterogeneity of AMRs will become increasingly commonplace. Companies like GreyOrange with their GreyMatter software solution and SVT Robotics with their SOFTBOT solution, offer open orchestration platforms enabling relatively straightforward integration and control of multiple robotic solutions from a variety of technology providers.

Most modern AMR software is built on the foundation of the Robot Operating System (ROS) developed by Eric Berger and Keenan Wyrobek while they were PhD students at Stanford University. ROS offers a straightforward set of frameworks for robot software developers with only a limited knowledge of robotics hardware. An update to ROS, known as ROS 2, was developed to simplify multirobot collaboration. A swarm system identifies the most appropriate robot with the capabilities to execute a specific task and assigns that task to the robot. When the AMR completes its task, it notifies the orchestration engine, which then marks the robot as available for the assignment of a new task. Most orchestration engines include sophisticated AI algorithms to plan travel paths, minimize congestion, optimize available capacity, and determine the most efficient location for idle robots to hover while waiting to be called upon to execute a new task.

AMR Vehicle Configurations

There are a multitude of vehicle configurations available from several different vendors, each falling into one of the following categories:

Type	Description
Shelf Mover AMR	Bots of varying sizes that can travel at speeds up to 2.5 m/s, with the ability to lift and move portable shelving units of varying weight classes, typically between 50 kg and 1,500 kg.
Case/Tote Mover AMR	Smaller bots with flat tops or roller conveyors, capable of moving cases or totes, offering an alternative to case conveyors.
Sorter AMR	Bots of varying sizes, heights, and load capacities, capable of moving and sorting single or double loads, with integrated conveyor segments or tilt-trays. Fully loaded, speeds as high as 2.5 m/s are achievable, some with load capacities as high as 100 kg.
Storage and Retrieval AMR	Bots with attached masts and temporary storage, capable of storing and retrieving totes or cases to and from standard racks. Fully loaded, they move at speeds up to 1.5 m/s, accessing storage locations as high as 10 meters.
Pallet Mover AMR	Larger flat-top bots, capable of moving pallets around a warehouse, often as an alternative to pallet conveyors. Speeds can reach 1.5 m/s with payloads up to 2,000 kg.
Robotic Picker AMR	Bots with attached articulated arms and grippers, capable of picking pallets, totes, cases, or eaches from onboard or external locations.
Forklift AMR	Similar to forklift AGVs but with Lidar and 3D visual navigation. They are able to lift and move pallet payloads up to 2,000 kg.
Collaborative AMR	Tote- and case-carrying bots equipped with a friendly user interface. Working collaboratively with humans, they are designed to follow or lead workers and to show up at the right time and location.

AMR Subsystems

The variation in configurable AMR-based solutions is nearly endless. It makes more sense to define the underlying subsystems that can be combined together to form specific solutions:

- Shelf-to-person picking: Originally deployed by Amazon with their Kiva solution, modular, four-sided shelving units are distributed throughout a facility. Products are stored in designated bins on shelves. When an item is ordered, a shelf-moving robot is dispatched by the orchestration engine to deliver the nearest shelving unit containing the product to a pick station. To aid the picker, a light adjacent to the bin holding the product illuminates. The picker follows the instructions displayed on a monitor and clicks a button after completing the pick. The robot, directed by the engine, then moves the shelving unit to a new temporary storage location. The location of each shelving unit regularly changes but the software tracks it at all times. Downstream operations (such as conveyance to consolidation areas) may be accomplished with case/tote mover AMRs or traditional conveyors.

- Follow-me or Follow-you pick-to-tote or pick-to-pallet: When static shelving is used to store products in a warehouse, pickers walk the aisles to pick the ordered products off shelving units as directed by lights or voice commands. These products might be cases that are picked to pallets or individual items that are picked to totes. As described in Chapter 6, this is known as PTG picking. The efficiency of the process can be improved by deploying collaborative robots or pallet-moving robots to follow or lead the worker to the next pick location. In the case of item picking, multiple totes are typically loaded on each robot. At each pick location, an illuminated light identifies the bin into which the picker is to place the item. When one or more of the robot's bins are full, the robot departs to a consolidation or packing area, and a new robot is dispatched to replace it. With case picking, all items are typically placed onto a single pallet carried on the body of the AMR.

- Tote-to-person picking: Similar to the operation of a shuttle system or a Mini Load ASRS, Storage and Retrieval AMRs retrieve totes or cases from static rack locations of varying heights and transport them to pick workstations. Any type of automated pick station may be used. When the order totes are complete, they are moved by collaborative AMRs or case/tote mover AMRs to a pack station. The partially depleted donor totes are moved by case/tote mover AMRs to a replenishment station or by Storage and Retrieval AMRs to return them to static rack locations. The orchestration engine controls all AMR selections, movements, and handoffs.

- Robotic case and eaches picking: In the scenarios described above, humans are responsible for the actual picking, whether walking up and down aisles or standing still at pick workstations. Robotic picking has also been piloted or used in many warehouses. Typically, the robotic arms are mounted on static platforms and deployed as GTR environments. Robotic Picker AMRs are beginning to enter the market as well, broadening the options to include RTG scenarios. Cases or totes are removed from shelves using vision-guided articulated arms attached to the body of a robot. Brightpick's Autopicker solution is an example. It stores both donor and order totes on its chassis, using a mounted robotic arm to move items from the donor tote to the order tote. After the pick is complete, the robot moves the donor tote back to the rack before it proceeds to retrieve a new one. When the order is complete, the AMR transports the order tote to a packing area or to a case/tote mover AMR which moves it to its next downstream location. In some cases, picking robots work in tandem with transport AMRs. The picking actuator is mounted to its platform and the transport AMR functions as it does in the follow-me scenario described above.

- Robotic sortation: Diverting items or cases into chutes or conveyor takeaways has traditionally been the job of linear or unit sorters. Sorter AMRs are cost-effective alternatives in some environments, particularly those that require very high flexibility of operation. A swarm of robots equipped with tilt-trays or conveyor tops can rapidly sort items into their designated locations as well. Several vendors are offering these subsystems today.

- Robotic pallet retrieval and movement: Forklift AMRs and Pallet Mover AMRs can offer advantages over a Unit Crane ASRS and pallet conveyors when it comes to flexibility and cost per storage position despite offering more limited throughput. Their primary role is to store and retrieve pallets and to move them to drop-off locations. An advantage is their ability to service multiple racks, rather than being confined to a single aisle. In case-picking environments, a forklift AMR might retrieve a pallet from a high-bay storage location and drop it onto a conveyor segment for subsequent pickup by a pallet-mover AMR. The pallet-mover might transport the pallet to a case-picking location where the cases are picked using a robotic case-picking AMR. The robot might subsequently pass the case to a case-mover AMR for movement to an order consolidation area.

Key Takeaways

- One benefit of AMR-based automation is the relative ease with which the various subsystems can be combined to form complete, end-to-end solutions. They are straightforward to install and configure and can easily be moved between warehouses.

- AMR-based solutions scale effectively, as additional AMRs may be leased during peak periods to increase throughput. They also have few single points of failure. If an AMR must be taken out of commission, the throughput degrades only proportionally.

- AMR orchestration software is highly complex but with homogeneous fleets of robots, WES integration work is relatively straightforward. The effort to integrate a WES with a broad range of bolted-down machines is usually more challenging and time consuming.
- AMR-based solutions may not be able to achieve the high-throughput levels demanded by some customers. Even when they can, the cost to achieve these levels may exceed that of more traditional solutions.
- Traffic congestion can be an issue with AMR-based solutions as throughput increases, potentially requiring an additional allocation of floor space.
- Special purpose ASRSs are able to store cases more densely, at higher levels, and can retrieve them more quickly than most AMRs equipped with vertical lift attachments.
- New AMR-based subsystems and solutions are being released by vendors regularly and limitations are being overcome. Each year, AMR-based solutions consume a larger slice of the rapidly growing warehouse automation market.

CHAPTER 12

Making Sense of All the Software

In automated warehousing systems, software is the glue that binds the hardware components together. The different software systems and the various machines typically come from a multitude of manufacturers. The better the design of the software and the more seamless the integration between components, the greater the reliability of the end-to-end solution. Software has become the great differentiator in automated warehouses, no longer the afterthought it once was.

The Challenge of Warehouse and Supply Chain Software

The core responsibility of warehouse and supply chain information systems is to manage and control the movement of goods that companies use when conducting business with customers, partners, and vendors. The systems must also integrate the movement of goods with a company's business structure and information flows.

This broad definition needs further refinement in order to understand the variety of systems that exist in the industry and how they may be assembled. They are more easily understood by analyzing two separate dimensions: The scope of the system and the functional level at which it operates.

The scope reflects the range of activities that a software system manages or controls. In the warehousing and supply chain industry, increasing levels of scope can be defined as follows:

- Sensor/Actuator: One or a small number of closely related sensors or actuators with local processing capabilities.

- Machine: A complete machine or a well-defined, semi-independent element of a machine that is provisioned and operated as a unit.
- Operating Cell: A group of machines that together perform a distinct function or operation in logistics processes, such as transportation, storage, packaging, and so on.
- Functional Area: One distinct functional area of the warehouse as described in Chapter 3: Inbound, Storage, Picking, Packing, Preparation, Sortation, Outbound.
- Facility: In the context of this book, the four walls housing the overall logistics flow, typically a warehouse, distribution center, or fulfillment center. When the focus is the broader logistics industry, this would include independently managed entities of the transportation network.
- Enterprise: A complete company including the logistics and fulfillment operation it controls.
- Supply Chain: The end-to-end fulfillment operations for a product, a group of products, or a market across multiple Enterprises.

The relevant functional levels at which a system operates are as follows:

- Equipment and Movement: Focused on monitoring the individual elements of equipment and their discrete movements such as the displacement of a shuttle to a predetermined position.
- Controls: Coordinated sequences of signals and movements that accomplish a well-defined goal like picking a tote from a slot.
- Operations: Instances of distinct material handling functions such as store, retrieve, pack, sort, and so on.
- Transactions: A commercial exchange between two parties such as Order, Delivery, Shipment, and so on.
- Business: The performance, metrics, and decisions of running a company, including its financials, customer satisfaction data, and so on.

We can map the traditional responsibilities of the software systems involved in supply chain automation and control against these two dimensions, as shown in Figure 12.1.

The resulting "alphabet soup" in the diagram reflects the challenge and complexity of the field and the fragmented solutions that vendors have provided over the years.

- PLC: Programmable Logic Controller is the name of the technology used to directly process sensor signals and to control actuators to perform and monitor individual equipment movements. These functions are also performed with industrial controllers running real-time operating systems.
- WCS: Warehouse Control Systems coordinate multiple movements into discrete tasks. They also interface and control the RF units (Voice and Handhelds) to direct workers and process their inputs.

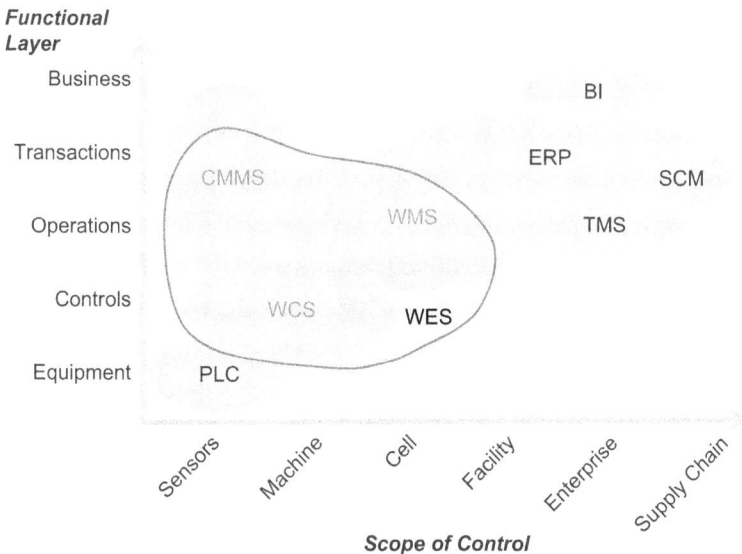

Figure 12.1 Software systems map displaying a broad range of supply chain operations and management systems

- WMS: Warehouse Management Systems are the original logistics information systems. Historically, they managed inventory, locations, pick lists, shipping, and receiving documentation. Although used standalone in manual operations, they also interact with WCSs to control automation. WMSs also overlap with ERPs in order management and product catalogs and act as the hub for EDI interaction with suppliers and downstream consumers.
- WES: Warehouse Execution Systems emerged in 2015 as a combination of WCS and WMS functionality, in response to customer demands for shorter fulfillment lead times and more reactive supply chains.
- CMMS: Computerized Maintenance Management Systems were created as an extension of Asset Management Systems, to support the operation and maintenance of automation equipment. With the availability of IoT technologies, these systems have access to real-time configuration, status, and alarms of the equipment.
- ERP: Enterprise Resource Planning systems started from financial systems and Manufacturing Resource Planning (MRP) systems. They have become the central system to support business processes across most functions in a company, including those related to logistics operations such as inventory control, order management, and supplier and customer management.
- TMS: Transportation Management Systems are dedicated to the planning and control of transportation tasks between supply chain nodes, including route and load planning. Similar to a CMMS, IoT technologies have connected these systems directly to vehicles and other logistics assets like containers and pallets.
- SCM: Supply Chain Management Systems specialize in coordinating activities across multiple nodes in a supply chain, managing multiechelon inventory levels, distributed order fulfillment, and other similar activities. To a large

extent, these systems have remained planning and batch oriented, with limited connection to real-time operations.

- BI: Business Intelligence systems and their associated data warehouses analyze historical data to create business reports, detect trends, and offer decision support. In the warehouse space, these systems are used for analysis and optimization of operations under the specialized discipline of Warehouse Optimization Software, which includes analytics, simulation, and more recently, AI and machine learning models.

The challenges that warehouse automation software faces arise from its positioning at the core of the overall systems landscape. The systems need to bridge real time, physical movements, and signals with the transaction-oriented environment of business processes. They also are central in the horizontal communication in supply chains, requiring extensive API and interface integration with ERPs, TMSs, and SCM systems.

PLCs, WCSs, WESs, and WMSs collectively constitute the brains of Warehouse Automation Systems. They integrate a broad range of technologies, with a multitude of complexities. Technologies range from real-time signal processing and control to robotic kinematics and dynamics, operations research and optimization, and distributed software and cloud systems.

Brief History of Warehouse Systems

The application of information systems in warehouse operations predates the use of modern automation within them. Early systems focused on making manual and paper processes more reliable and to improve picking productivity. Manual picking strategies such as zone picking, pick-to-cart, or batch picking, described in Chapter 6, were implemented with physical pick lists that would be printed for pickers by the central office. Pick and pack lists were generated from a batch of orders and provided pickers and packers with work for a whole shift or half a shift in "waves" of work that fulfilled a predefined batch of orders. Initial WMSs would automate the generation of these lists from uploaded orders, enabling improved optimization.

At this early stage in the evolution of automated warehousing systems, material handling equipment was used to transport full totes in pick-to-conveyor processes but they were mostly disassociated from the planning and execution of pick and pack operations.

The introduction of RF terminals, pick-to-light systems, and later, voice-enabled terminals, removed the need for printed pick-and-pack instructions in warehouses. At the same time, networked printers and PCs eliminated the need for preprinted labels. These new capabilities required dedicated systems to manage and control them, leading to the creation of WCSs. Initially, these systems dealt with small subsets of operations within the warehouse (e.g., packing, labeling, shipping, or picking sortation). Control of the movement of goods was enabled with photoelectric sensors to detect the presence of goods and to identify them using barcode readers. These developments, together with the RF terminals used by operators, allowed the WCS to make routing decisions and to coordinate the flow of goods.

The local processing power of PLCs and their relative ease of programming made them affordable for use in warehouses, enabling the introduction of automated storage and retrieval systems and increasingly sophisticated control of equipment like sortation machines. All this equipment became connected to the WCS layer, expanding the reach and footprint of warehousing systems.

Planning and sequencing of tasks in the warehouse followed the "wave" fulfillment strategies that were established earlier. WMSs handled inventory, locations, and resources, and produced wave-plans that the WCS would execute, directing the movement of equipment and operators. The information flow in these systems, as illustrated in Figure 12.2, is top-down, with higher-level systems creating plans and sending instructions to lower levels. Lower levels report on the results of the operations and signal any incidences that arise from the shop floor.

The pressure created by e-commerce to shorten delivery times and the change in order composition to just a few items per order made top-down planning and wave fulfillment practices less competitive. The initial response of implementers was to create smaller, more frequent waves (micro-waves), keeping the overall structure of the information systems intact. Eventually, the "top-down" planning and control structure proved incapable of delivering on the demands imposed by e-commerce.

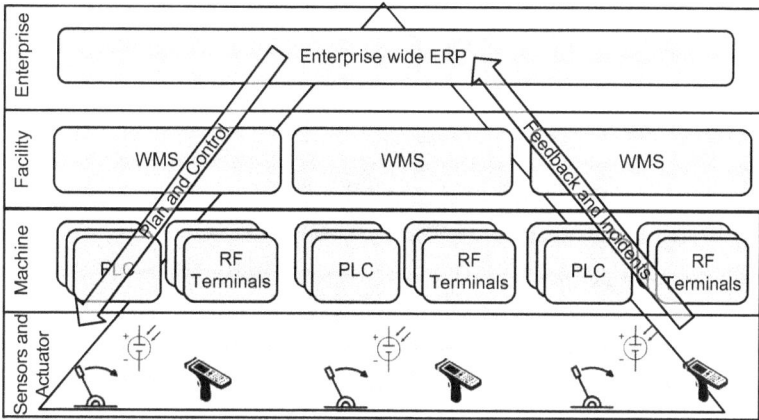

Figure 12.2 Traditional information flows in batch- or wave-oriented systems

In response to conditions on the warehouse floor, the WCS needed to develop planning capabilities of its own, to handle exceptions and to replan work in near real-time. Eventually, a new paradigm for order planning and fulfillment emerged with "waveless" algorithms that processed orders the moment they arrived.

Waveless fulfillment follows the principles of Just-In-Time and Agile manufacturing pioneered by Toyota in its Toyota Production System. In these environments, activities are executed in response to "horizontal" demand and availability signals, in contrast with the "vertical" plan and dispatch structure used in traditional MRP systems. The impact of this shift in operational practice was that WMS planning and WCS control functions blended into an agile, real-time, closed, control loop. A new generation of systems emerged which became the modern integrated WES, as shown in Figure 12.3.

WESs have facilitated the integration of increasingly sophisticated equipment like autonomous vehicles and robots. Their ability to sense their environment and to receive input in real time made them a good match for implementing new agile fulfillment algorithms. Agile algorithms can maximize the efficiency of smart equipment, which can dramatically improve the ROI of automation investments.

The evolution of operations and information systems has not slowed down, if anything it has accelerated due to the continued advancements in smart equipment and the ongoing growth of e-commerce expectations.

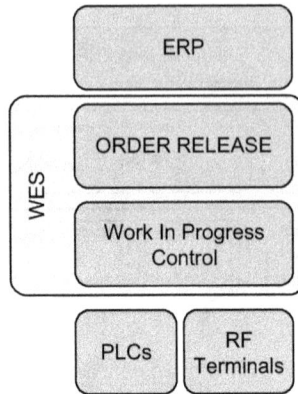

Figure 12.3 Warehouse execution systems combine the WMS and WCS layers

Two areas of development are particularly active. The application of ML and AI, and the expansion of fulfillment planning to cover multiple warehouses or fulfillment centers.

ML and AI are being applied to make equipment smarter, more able to react to exceptions in the operation and to enable equipment to operate in less structured environments. For example, vision systems, coupled with flexible robotic arms controlled by AI systems, can pick goods off a conveyor without requiring strict alignment or singulation. AMRs can chart their route in a warehouse without the need for wire guides or laser locators and can avoid dynamic obstacles, including people, reducing the need for safety exclusion zones.

An explosion in product variety and the creation of smaller warehouses near consumption points require the fulfillment of orders from multiple locations in a coordinated way. This is enabled by deploying software in the cloud, increasingly reliable networks, and the interconnection of technologies that support the "Internet of Things." These systems, which have visibility across multiple warehouses and coordinate fulfillment activities across them, are bringing to the multifacility realm the agile, reactive practices already successful in waveless fulfillment. They add a layer of control for distributed fulfillment, logistics, and inventory processes across an enterprise as shown in Figure 12.4, relieving the ERP from these coordination tasks.

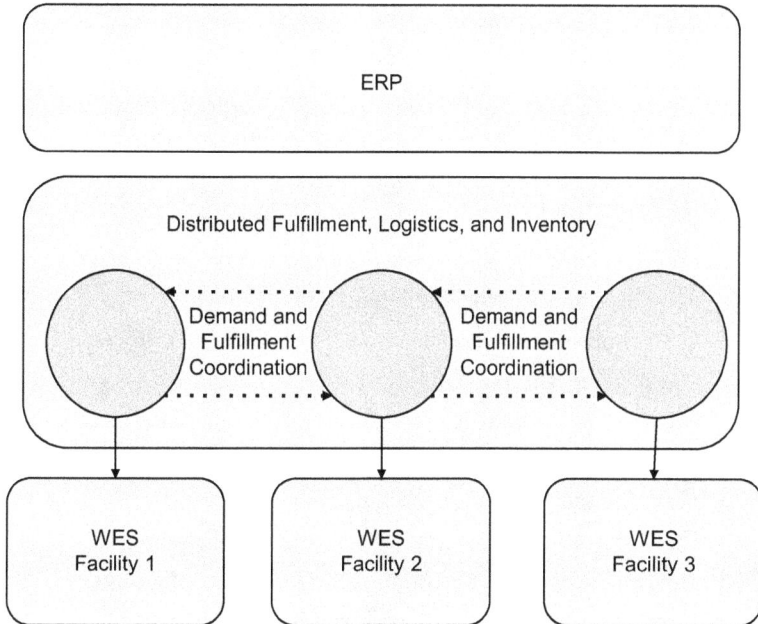

Figure 12.4 Distributed logistics, fulfillment, and inventory forms a specialized layer between the ERP and WESs in individual facilities

The Warehouse Execution System

Functionality

Warehouse Execution Systems provide functionality that directs and supports activities taking place in warehouses and fulfillment centers. Their functionality includes:

- Acquisition of real-time signals and the control of material handling movements.
- Coordination of tasks within the equipment that performs a material handling function or synchronization across functions.
- Administration and management of the resources available to the warehouse for fulfillment operations, including labor, equipment, locations, and inventory.

- Planning and optimization of end-to-end operations in a warehouse, including receiving, storage, fulfillment, and other enabling functions like counting and moving inventory.
- Handling exceptions when executing fulfillment plans, replanning, and taking corrective actions where appropriate.
- Receiving orders from ERP systems, e-commerce sites, or other demand origination systems, prioritizing the orders, and releasing them for fulfillment.
- Collect information associated with the fulfillment processes and relaying it to the ERP or other order-generating systems.
- Monitoring equipment and managing faults, maintenance windows, and activities, integrating the resulting status into planning and tracking functions.
- Operation and administration of each piece of equipment and of the complete system, for provisioning, configuration, performance measurement, and security management.
- Providing access to its historical records for analytics systems to use in business intelligence functions or for continuous analysis and improvement of standard processes executing in the warehouse.

Behavior

In effective fulfillment operations, as soon as an order is accepted by the e-commerce site, it is placed in a pending order queue. From this point forward, the order progresses through the fulfillment process.

Release and planning can be done in groups of orders or as individual orders, depending on whether the operation is set up to work in waves or through continuous fulfillment. Orders are released according to committed delivery dates and a varied set of optimization parameters. Released orders are assigned the inventory that will be used to fulfill them, which also determines the pick locations. Selection of inventory and locations in modern systems depends on the current state of the equipment and on orders already in process. Picking instructions are then sent to equipment or operators through the control software and scheduled for execution. Subsequent operations of consolidation, packaging, and labeling are scheduled to minimize wait times and to maximize the productivity of the warehouse. As operations are complete, the control software collects the signals from the equipment or RF terminals and updates the state of the order until it is shipped. In the case of unexpected incidents or deviations with respect to the planned tasks, the control software reacts to correct them by replanning locally or by communicating with a higher-level controller. If the deviation cannot be corrected, perhaps because there is no actual inventory, the incident is reported back to the ordering system.

Warehouse Execution Systems also monitor and manage the automation equipment in the warehouse. They receive signals from the equipment to determine potential failures and use diagnostic logic, potentially including machine learning, to determine the best time to perform maintenance activities. By taking advantage of the integrated nature of a WES, fulfillment operations can be rerouted to bypass equipment that is out of service. When it recovers, work is rerouted to it once again.

Anatomy

Warehouse Execution Systems have become the core systems supporting most of the functions described above and most are built in a modular way. Modularity in WESs serves two purposes: (1) it allows them to easily adapt their deployment to support multiple configurations of physical layout, equipment, and processes; (2) it enables developers and vendors to create and maintain the system more easily and efficiently. Figure 12.5 shows the key modules of a WES and how they relate to each other. Not all WES software systems include all of these modules. This reference model is conceptual in order to describe the operation of these systems more clearly.

The WES manages and controls the activities of the warehouse in response to inputs received from ERP, SCM, and TMS systems, such as fulfillment orders and transportation delivery information. It replies back with receipt confirmations, inventory counts, resource usage, labor statistics, as well as any exceptions related to these activities. In addition, it sends regular data updates to data warehouses for historical recording and analysis. This is done through the Host Interface module, where it

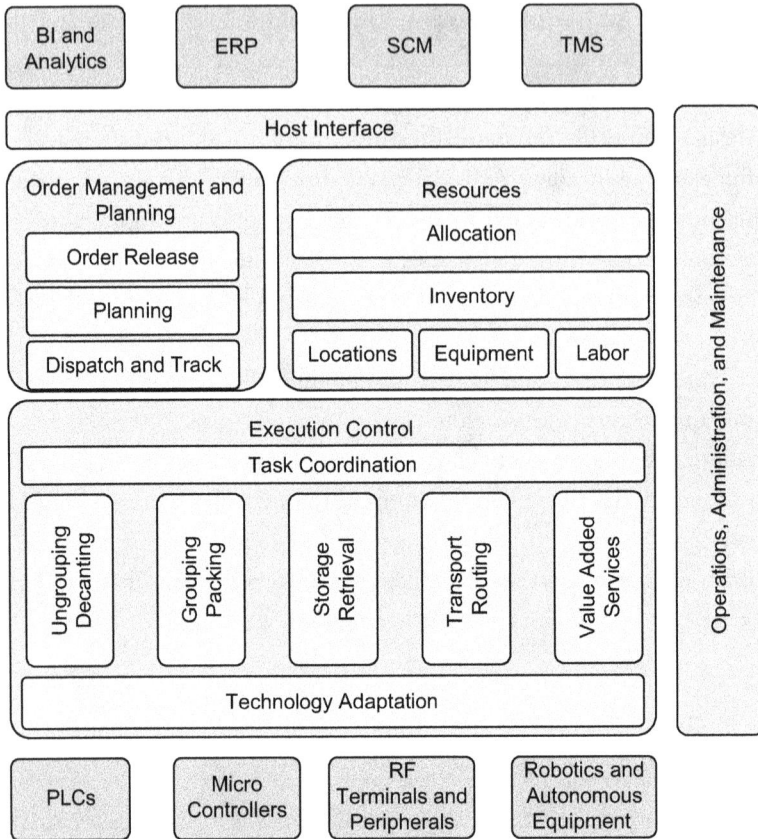

Figure 12.5 WES functional anatomy

receives requests from external systems and dispatches them to the appropriate functional module. Additionally, it sends messages to the host system to notify it of any relevant updates in the warehouse. Finally, this module is responsible for adapting the communication protocols used by external systems.

The Order Management and Planning module decides how orders are released to the warehouse. It uses information from the Resources module to determine the status and allocation of inventory, equipment, and personnel. Orders considered for release have resources allocated to them and related operations are sequenced and scheduled via a plan to fulfill them. The planned operations are dispatched for execution once they become feasible (e.g., the resources become available and all preconditions are met).

The resources module acts as a bookkeeper for the system, recording the status and availability of the resources available for order fulfillment or other activities. An operation planned as part of order fulfillment may involve performing multiple tasks in a prescribed sequence by different operators or equipment. The Task Coordination Module decomposes each operation into its individual tasks and uses the specialized modules in varying material handling functions to perform them. These specialized modules in turn dispatch discrete instructions to equipment and labor using the appropriate controller software, accessed through dedicated interfaces and protocols.

At the same time that this top-down flow of instructions takes place, the lower layers of the system, PLCs and RF terminals are transmitting signals upward to the control modules. These signals are used to update the state of resources, evaluate the progress of orders, or take corrective actions when incidents occur. This flow of events enables a WES to implement near-real-time planning, dispatching, and execution. This differentiates a WES from the top-down control prevalent in earlier MRP systems and wave-based WMSs.

The final element in the functional blocks is Operation, Administration, and Maintenance, which affects all the layers in the system. It is responsible for configuring and provisioning all the equipment and receives health and performance metrics to detect actual or predicted failures, schedule maintenance interventions, and update the configuration as needed. Analytics is not included in the description of the WES, despite metrics and performance analysis being an essential part of modern operations. The reason is that these systems typically integrate warehouse and fulfillment operations with additional data from e-commerce sites, sales, and financials, and are implemented outside the scope of the WES. A WES contributes to this function by providing access to its operational data stores. With the increasing use of microservices-based architectures, and increasingly sophisticated information structures in the WES, direct access to its databases is rarely granted. Instead, best practices favor a dedicated "data stream" interface that the WES makes available for use by the data warehouse. Multiple technologies are available to build these streaming connectors and to publish the data collected by the WES in a safe and secure way.

Technologies

The emergence of Warehouse Execution Systems has occurred in the context of the technologies that enable them. Modern WESs combine the functionality of traditional enterprise information systems with real-time control. This is only possible because of the maturity of software frameworks that simplify the complexity of communications, computation, storage, and integration. As nonexhaustive examples of these frameworks, Kubernetes simplifies the deployment and operation of distributed systems, Representational State Transfer (REST) and binary Remote Procedure Call (RPC) communication protocols make standardization of integration points and interaction between services inside the system reliable and trouble free. Cloud-deployed databases have made those technologies accessible without the specialized knowledge that was previously required for development, deployment, and operation of these systems.

For WESs to operate reliably and without constant supervision, the algorithms and decision making in planning, task dispatching, and equipment monitoring need to consider a much more complex operating environment that integrates real-time conditions with complex enterprise order fulfillment. These algorithms are increasingly supported by machine learning and artificial intelligence technologies to help cover most operating conditions.

Advanced Trends

In warehouse automation, as in many other technology industries, software is one of the areas showing the most rapid pace of change and innovation. This trend is compounded by industry-specific changes driven by e-commerce and the pressure to reduce lead times driving additional innovation in operating processes and optimization algorithms.

Data collected by a WCS or WES is now made available to operators in data warehouse and analytics applications specific to logistics activities. These applications, while they resemble enterprise BI systems in their architecture, are closely integrated with operational systems. They offer much more rapid analysis than traditional BI and come with predefined metrics and algorithms that reflect the best practices of the industry. Warehouse managers can now look at these results in near-real time and make decisions that affect operations directly, instead of having to wait for offline reports before making changes. Analytics are also being enhanced with online simulation capabilities that allow decision makers to execute "what-if" scenarios to test alternative changes and decision outcomes before they are formally implemented. AI and ML can be leveraged to ingest these data streams and simulation inputs to identify and propose operations optimizations. Large ML models have not seen widespread adoption in the industry yet but large logistics operators are starting to deploy them in guarded, proprietary environments.

The pressure for shorter fulfillment times is leading the transformation from wave/batch to waveless/continuous fulfillment operations. This transformation is enabled by the availability of distributed computing architectures with asynchronous processing capabilities (e.g., agent systems or microservices) which are helping to drive their adoption.

Key Takeaways

- Supply Chain Automation and Control systems span a very broad scope, from sensors and actuators to multicompany supply chain orchestration. They touch all levels of operations from individual signals to business metrics and results.
- The software industry provides a number of specialized solutions to help minimize inherent integration complexities and operational inefficiencies.
- Within the warehouse, information systems were introduced as an extension of manual processes, taking their best practices and automating them (e.g., waves and batch picking).
- With the availability of real-time controls and online capabilities, and due to the pressure of e-commerce demands, the management and control layers in a warehouse are merging into integrated Warehouse Execution Systems (WES) that support real-time algorithms such as waveless fulfillment.
- In the coming years, we can expect further integration of real-time operations, application of AI and ML capabilities, and the expansion of systems to support multifacility management through cloud systems.

CHAPTER 13

The Evolution of Automated Fulfillment

Any attempt to peer into the future is risky business and needs to be taken with a healthy dose of caution. E-commerce has been the most visible driver of change in distribution and fulfillment operations over the past 10 years, and it continues to evolve under the pressure of changing demographics and consumer habits.

It Is About Demographics

Populations are getting older, more urban, and wealthier, and these changes are having a profound impact on consumption patterns and labor characteristics.

In the last 50 years, the age distribution has shifted heavily toward older demographics, and according to a recent UN Population Division projection, it will continue doing so over the course of the next 50 years. Aging consumers, with reduced mobility and energy, put a premium on convenience services. So far, most companies have responded with extremely labor-intensive "personal shopper" services. Clearly, this is only the first iteration of solutions for this demographic. Automation technologies in micro-fulfillment and last-leg delivery are beginning to emerge in response to this demand.

On the labor front, distribution and fulfillment activities are local by nature and cannot be offshored. According to a United Nations population study conducted in 2022, population aging is even more pronounced in advanced, wealthier countries where higher levels of consumption take place. The labor pool in these countries, typified by the United States, is similarly aging. The percentage of men over 65 in the labor pool, which has increased over the past 20 years, is comparable to the increase caused by WWII after more than 100 years of decline.

An older labor force in advanced countries, with strict work safety standards, is pushing industry to find technologies to assist workers in performing physically demanding tasks, or to eliminate these tasks altogether.

Another trend that has accelerated in the last 10 years, is the increased concentration of the population in dense, urban areas. As seen in Figure 13.1, the number of people in the world living in urban areas exceeded the number living in rural areas in 2008, and the gap is expected to grow despite the presence of COVID disruptions, as shown in the 2022 UN World Cities Report.

Urbanization itself is not uniform, with large urban metropolises being the predominant geographies where populations concentrate. In this context, distribution and fulfillment operations are forced to compete for real estate with residential and retail uses of land. Warehouses face additional constraints because they are forced to remain in preexisting buildings, with limited flexibility of layout compared to greenfield projects.

Distribution and fulfillment operations need to adopt technologies that allow them to store goods more densely to minimize real estate costs at locations that are closer to their customers. They also need to optimize for smaller batches/waves in both shipping and replenishment, to support higher inventory rotations using smaller delivery vehicles that visit customers more frequently. Finally, any technology that is used must be able

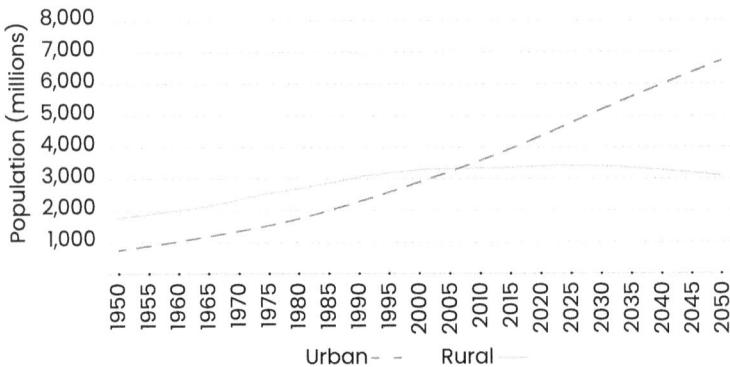

Figure 13.1 Urban and rural population of the world (1950–2030), UN World Cities Report 2022

to accommodate the highly constrained and variable deployment environments of preexisting facility infrastructures, without a corresponding increase in the cost of engineering customizations.

Aging and urbanization have occurred at the same time as the emergence of the largest middle class in history. According to information collated by the Maddison Historical Statistics Project, the relative disparity in Gross Domestic Product (GDP) between advanced economies and developing economies has reduced by an order of magnitude in the past 70 years. Around 1950, the ratio between the highest and lowest GDP per capita was about 30 times, and by 2018, that ratio was just over 3 times.

As reported by the World Bank in 2022, the percentage of the population living under the poverty line is also on track to be halved since the early 1980s, together with a pronounced reduction in illiteracy. Illiteracy has largely disappeared in developed economies, where the average schooling has climbed from 6 to 9 years, to 12 to 15 years.

Changes in income have created an increased demand for goods around the world. At the same time, local labor for low-skilled warehouse jobs has become scarcer, creating the perfect storm of supply versus demand.

Information Is Power

While these large-scale demographic changes are straining distribution networks around the world, the emergence of the information economy has shifted the power from manufacturers, distributors, and retailers, to consumers.

E-commerce has reached approximately one-fifth of all retail sales in the United States, shifting control from the retailer to the consumer. Amazon is the dominant e-commerce retailer with over 40 percent of the total market in the United States. It retains this position through rapid delivery and accuracy, while maintaining price competitiveness with leading retailers like Walmart and Target. The inability of Amazon to raise prices versus its competitors, despite their advantages, illustrates that competing e-commerce retailers are just a Google search away, and consumers face almost no cost of switching. Consumer expectations, with this new found power, are forcing retailers to shorten fulfillment times, down to hours in some markets, and to offer a nearly unlimited number of products. The Amazon marketplace contains approximately 350 million different SKUs. The combination of fulfillment times and the number of available SKUs has had an enormous impact on the complexity of warehousing and fulfillment operations.

Performance metrics for warehousing and fulfillment are shifting from operational metrics like cost per unit shipped, to metrics like fulfillment lead time, order accuracy, and out-of-stock incidents. The new measurements are more focused on customer satisfaction and revenue than they are on cost. At the same time, warehouses are forced to carry a broader array of products than they did before, forcing them to change their putaway and picking methodologies as traditional strategies for handling fast and slow movers don't work anymore.

Change Is Accelerating and Creating Uncertainty

All these changes in consumer demographics and behavior, as well as the competitive response from retailers, are creating an environment of rapid change and variability in demand. The traditional operational response to uncertainty has been to create fulfillment buffers by carrying inventory in distribution centers, or increasing planning horizons, requiring customers to place orders in advance. Variability has been met by maintaining manual processes even if an automated solution would be more efficient in some of the operational environments.

Automation Technology Is Evolving to Address the New Landscape

Traditional automation technologies, with their large up-front capital costs and relative lack of operational flexibility, are not yet able to support these emerging needs. Even Amazon, with its leading capabilities, relies heavily on manual operations, having surpassed one million employees in the United States alone in February 2022.

In the innovation race to support the evolution of fulfillment, warehouse automation has also accelerated its technology cycles. Taking a historical perspective for ASRS systems, it took several decades for the technology to move from large automated cranes for pallet storage to lightweight cranes for cases and cartons, and finally to shuttle systems to support Goods-to-Person operations. Shuttles, initially introduced in the early 2000s, are essentially multiprocessor storage systems. Since then, the innovation around storage systems for fulfillment has included several variations of shuttles that can change aisles or levels, or depart the storage unit altogether. Alternative systems like AutoStore or Kiva also address high density or specialized layout requirements.

The rate of innovation is benefiting from a broad set of technology developments in other fields. Computing and communication capabilities, following Moore's law for decades by doubling their speed and halving their cost every two years, have reached a point where they can be considered ubiquitous and easy to apply. The explosion of IoT standards and connected devices running on micro-kernel operating systems enable "smart" equipment, providing real-time sensing and control to the material flow in the warehouse from every automation component. The cost of these components has plunged thanks to technologies contained in consumer-oriented markets like smartphones and home automation systems. While an industrial environment is much more demanding in terms of reliability and durability, the low cost of sensors and processing enables adequate levels of performance through redundancy and the replaceability of components.

On the other end of the computing spectrum, the availability and maturity of cloud platforms puts enterprise-scale computing within the reach of companies and facilities that are too small to support dedicated, on-premise control systems. Cloud and Software-as-a-Service (SaaS) systems are now the mainstream deployment approach for enterprise systems like ERP, Customer Relationship Management (CRM), and Data Warehouses (DW), with an increasing penetration into more operational areas like WMS. The last processes to adopt the cloud are real-time or near real-time equipment management and control software systems like a WES or a WCS. Adoption of cloud deployments in these processes started with monitoring and maintenance applications that collect data and provide alerts and diagnostics to support personnel. There is an active push by upstarts in the field to create cloud applications for the direct control of operational tasks through hybrid systems. They use local controllers for individual equipment elements and cloud orchestration backends to manage cells at the facility or multifacility level.

Although there is no hard data available for a rigorous assessment, IoT, containerized computing, and cloud environments have slashed the cost of developing software for automation to a fraction of what it used to be. The lower barrier to building management and execution systems creates an opportunity for small independent software vendors, and even logistics operators, to develop specialized systems tailored to specific operational models and use cases.

As equipment elements and cells become smarter, the information streams they generate become richer and more commonplace. These information streams include structured event notifications as well as unstructured data like vision and environmental sensor signals. It is increasingly difficult to make good use of that information using traditional data analysis techniques. Here again, technologies emerging from consumer applications in AI and ML have evolved rapidly during the last few years and are finding applications in industrial environments for predictive diagnosis, maintenance, performance analysis, and optimization.

Machine vision systems deserve special attention among technologies that have recently impacted fulfillment operations. They have matured enough to match human dexterity in some of the challenging picking and packing tasks that have defied automation in the past. Machine vision is now used in production settings in a variety of cases. The most mature applications are the ones that recognize products on shelves or pallets and those that identify empty spaces in storage areas. This information is used to improve the accuracy of inventory counts, to direct human operators for picking or put-away, or as quality control gates for operations performed by humans (e.g., inspection of pick bins before and after the pick). Another common application of machine vision is in autonomous vehicle navigation, improving the costs of LiDAR-based systems, and simplifying their commissioning and configuration. Application of vision is a key driver in the adoption of AMRs in warehouse environments as they drive the deployment cost of these systems down to a range that they become practical aids for human pickers. Human pickers are exceedingly good at eye-hand coordination. Self-guided AMR vehicles allow pickers to dedicate more time to this specific task by relieving them of the need to take long walks to deliver bins. The combination of human pickers with AMR vehicles is beginning to compete with traditional pick-to-conveyor operations, minimizing or removing the conveyor altogether and providing more flexibility in the process. The additional flexibility is used to enable a broader catalog of products or to absorb the seasonal variation in product mix and volume.

The more advanced applications of vision systems are usually in combination with articulated arm robots for case or each picking, and with the guidance of robots for pallet building, particularly for mixed-pallet construction. Vision assisted each-picking is at the forefront of innovation and is currently evolving. While it doesn't always compete with human eye-hand coordination, it is becoming economically feasible in tightly controlled environments, which provides a feedback loop and accelerates technology development.

A new class of automation vendors focused on best-of-breed functional modules has emerged. Traditional automation projects were predominantly designed with equipment from a single vendor, driven by vertically integrated systems vendors. More recently, dedicated storage modules and robotic cells from multiple vendors are being combined into a single system, in a way that is reminiscent of the computer industry in the 80s and 90s. It went from integrated suppliers like IBM and DEC to an ecosystem of component suppliers conforming to industry standard architectures. This transformation is far from complete in the automation industry but most of the elements are already present. An accelerated adoption of standard networking protocols and operating systems makes the inter-operation of elements from multiple vendors easier. Higher-level operations (e.g., storage commands or routing directives) don't have unified standards yet. Instead, they are being driven by proprietary protocols defined by system integrators, equipment vendors, or the logistics operators themselves. Amazon, with its "Amazon Fulfillment Technologies" group, is a major driver of technology interoperability but they keep their development tightly guarded, not even sharing it openly with their systems suppliers.

Evolution of Operational Models

At the same time that automation-enabling component technologies are changing, operational models for distribution and fulfillment are also changing. The traditional models were vertically controlled operations, typically built to service a retailer's store footprint. They were predominantly based on a hub-and-spoke mix of in-house and 3PL operation centers. Homogeneous pallets flowed from distribution centers to fulfillment centers and mixed-pallets flowed from fulfillment centers to retail stores. Relatively light-weight coordination between these centers was acceptable for business cycles that were measured in weeks and planning horizons that were measured in months. Coordination was achieved mostly through EDI-based messaging. The initial impact of e-commerce was on the fulfillment centers that now had to fulfill both store orders and direct consumer orders. With shortened delivery times and increased product variability and sourcing, new operational models were required.

The most visible new operational model is the one that Amazon successfully implemented in its fulfillment centers. Amazon has eliminated the two-tier distribution and fulfillment network in favor of a single layer. Fulfillment centers receive pallets directly from multiple sources (manufacturers, other distributors, independent marketplace participants), break them up into units, and store them as individual products for direct order fulfillment. These centers build direct-to-consumer packages that are handed over to a parcel delivery operation, be it Amazon's own or a 3rd party. Amazon benefits from its complete visibility and control of the resources and inventory at its centers. With this information, its computing systems make decisions not only within each center but also across centers, to optimize product availability and delivery times. The two main downsides of the model are as follows:

- It is very asset intensive. The state of the operation (congestion, truck capacity, etc.) is achieved through total ownership and control.
- It is designed for e-commerce fulfillment. Most orders consist of just a single-item and rarely more than three items. Orders are always packed into parcel manageable packages, never onto pallets or other larger units.

The Amazon Fulfillment Engine (AFE) assets and processes are accessible to Amazon e-commerce solutions and all participating merchants. Companies like ShipMonk, ShipBob, and Deliverr (acquired by Flexport in 2023) offer Fulfillment-as-a-Service (FaaS) solutions. They aim to provide robust fulfillment services to other e-retailers. Their model is similar to Amazon's in that they control, and in many cases own, the assets they use to provide their services.

An alternative fulfillment model to the asset intensive one pioneered by Amazon is one where independent actors collaborate in the fulfillment of a customer order. These models have been promoted by e-shopping hubs such as Alibaba, Shopify, or Google Shopping. Shopify developed a storefront for an ecosystem of merchants, with each of them arranging fulfillment independently. Google Shopping partnered with retailers and acted as a consolidation and last-mile delivery partner. Alibaba is a special case in the Chinese market with strong ties to parcel delivery companies that were leveraged by its participating merchants. The main obstacle to success of these models, from a supply chain operations perspective, is the absence of widely adopted standards for fulfillment center coordination. This remains an unsolved problem in the industry and an opportunity for innovation. The relevant analogy is how data networks evolved from being centrally controlled by national or monopolistic telecommunications carriers to a decentralized aggregation of independently managed networks that adhere to common routing, congestion, and signaling standards. We believe that standards will emerge in the distribution market as well and will enable true marketplaces and fulfillment ecosystems. While it is not certain what models will prevail, the inescapable conclusion is that warehouse operations will not be confined to a single center, rather they will be performed at a network level through a combination of distribution centers, fulfillment centers, parcel delivery services, and cross-facility shipments. It is in this context that the future of automation and information systems needs to be imagined.

Smart Automation for Flexible Operations

Demands placed on fulfillment networks due to variability, labor scarcity, order lead times, and a large number of SKUs with a long tail of slow-moving items are common to distribution and fulfillment centers.

From an automation perspective, flexible automation in the form of AMRs, standardization of technologies, and sensors are becoming more competitive with traditional convey/sort-based PTG systems and ASRS-based GTP systems. The big differentiator between distribution and fulfillment centers is the availability of space. Distribution centers tend to be located in low-cost real estate areas, while fulfillment centers, by necessity, are closer to consumers, and as such bear higher real estate costs.

Fulfillment operations near consumers, with their focus on density, cannot afford the walkways and fire safety spaces that PTG operations require. With the adoption of MFCs, the preferred design is built around a central "storage engine" that is fully automated and delivers donor totes to pick stations. Shuttles, cubic systems, and other 3D storage machines will provide the central storage engines, sending totes to pick stations operated by workers. It will be interesting to see the evolution of these operations, either by replacing the picking tasks with specialized robots at the output of the storage engine or by transforming the storage engines into each-based engines by embedding the picking robot into the core of the engine. Robotic picking cells have been in active development for a number of years and while not ready for widespread deployment, they are already effective in environments that control the variation of the products to pick. Advances in artificial intelligence and machine learning are quickly expanding the range of conditions under which these cells are effective, which will make them more common in increasingly complex automation projects.

Next-generation distribution centers will be structured more frequently around fleets of AMRs to leverage their deployment flexibility or to increase the productivity of picking operations. Traditional pick-to-tote processes, utilizing either zone picking, batch picking, or order picking, will use AMRs to eliminate worker travel times, allowing the workers to focus on picking products. The same technology can be used to increase the flexibility and reach of pick-to-conveyor processes, as AMRs can reach larger areas and can be reconfigured on the fly. Goods-to-Person systems use AMRs to bring inventory sets (e.g., mobile shelves or individual totes) to operators for picking. These systems may not reach the picking efficiencies of other GTP systems but they are much more adaptable to variations in throughput, products, and available space.

Most of these innovations are designed to work collaboratively with workers, eliminating activities unrelated to their eye-hand coordination. They also eliminate physically demanding tasks, allowing a broader demographic to perform picking tasks effectively. Human-robot collaborative environments demand high levels of safety on the automation side. Ubiquitous sensors and local control processing power have enabled the required safety levels to be met while eliminating the physical barriers needed in more traditional automation environments. Robotic picking in open, less structured environments poses higher demands on the automation technologies than the picking station scenario described above. ML and AI advances are improving this situation as well. In addition to challenges that are common to robotic picking cells, mobile picking must contend with limitations of power, mechanical balance, and product reachability. Product reachability for humans is trivially solved by using two hands (hold a tote/case with one hand, reach inside with the other). This is due to our combination of visual and tactile sensing ability, the 27 degrees of freedom available to each human hand, and the 7 degrees of freedom available to each arm. Robotic manipulator technology is far from achieving these levels of dexterity, even with the most advanced actuators. Although picking does not require equivalent dexterity, the less structured the environment and the higher the variety of products to be picked, the more difficult it is for automation to replace humans in picking operations. When picking takes place in tight spaces, with varied product shapes and rigidity, or with a need to manipulate multiple objects, it will continue to be extremely difficult to automate.

Control and Operations

In addition to new technologies, the industry is also undergoing a transformation in the way that warehouses define and assign tasks to operators or automation equipment. Traditional warehouse management and control systems have relied on tasks executed in waves of work with many orders in each wave. A batch approach to order fulfillment allowed the planning of tasks to be separate from their execution, and as a result, to have separate systems for management and real-time control. The separation was enabled by the typical order/fulfillment cadence of repeat orders being fulfilled weekly or even less frequently. To some extent, the separation was also required because of limited computing and communication capacity that was unable to dynamically replan quickly enough in response to real-time events on the shop floor. New order release policies, collectively known as waveless fulfillment, integrate planning and integration into a continuous feedback loop, merging the functionality of WMS and WCS systems into a new generation of WESs. Waveless control policies, as described in a seminal paper by Jérémie Gallien and Théophane Weber at MIT, result in shorter lead times with lower variability than wave-based policies, by using real-time state information from the shop floor. Ubiquitous sensors, computing, and communication capabilities have enabled this revolution in warehouse operations, regardless of the mix of manual and automated processes deployed.

It Is a Fulfillment Network

The breadth of products demanded by consumers cannot be fulfilled by a single warehouse no matter how large it is. Even Amazon fulfillment centers, handling tens of millions of SKUs each, are pooled together. Merchants need to rely on multiple inventory locations, either their own or their suppliers' or partners' to be able to offer variety to consumers. Order fulfillment must coordinate tasks across multiple warehouses to offer a seamless delivery to customers. A failure to do so will impact customer loyalty and ultimately revenue. The enabling technology for controlling multiple warehouses is cloud-based logistics systems. Leading retailers have developed their own cloud systems. Independent software vendors are lagging behind these proprietary implementations but cloud systems are already available from ERP suppliers such as Oracle, SAP, or NetSuite. Adoption of cloud-based systems will increase as the industry resolves the two main obstacles blocking their adoption. The first obstacle is the increased latency that they introduce in terms of the controller response time. Currently, it is reasonably safe to rely on cloud response times of one to three seconds but automated equipment requires latencies in the tens of milliseconds. The discrepancy needs to be absorbed by control nodes deployed on-premise that act as local delegates of the WES. The second obstacle is the increased risk of downtime due to network disconnections and "Internet weather." Similar to latency, this can be mitigated by using local control stations. These hybrid, on-premise/cloud systems are significantly more complex than full on-premise or full cloud systems. Virtualization technologies enable a path forward to realize these solutions.

Warehouse Automation advanced significantly, though somewhat slowly and linearly, over the past fifty years. It's now time to buckle our collective seatbelts, as the world of robotics and AI, coupled with a growing and increasingly demanding market, will drive the level of innovation and growth to levels we have never seen before.

Key Takeaways

- Changes in demographics, consumer behavior, and the digitalization of commerce are driving profound change in the distribution and fulfillment operations of warehouses.
- The automation industry has responded with flexible automation technologies using robotics, advanced sensors, machine learning, and artificial intelligence.
- New automation technologies, coupled with warehouses operating in a "waveless" continuous fulfillment mode, lead to higher expectations in accuracy and delivery lead times.
- Cloud systems enable fulfillment to be coordinated across multiple facilities, creating networked fulfillment systems that can handle larger product variations while maintaining shorter delivery times.

Appendixes

Appendix 1: Industry Players

Warehouse and logistics automation is a mature, complex industry with many players that play different roles. In this appendix, we classify the participants into some categories to help orient the reader. We don't provide descriptions of the companies mentioned as more current information for the reader is only one Internet search away.

Large, Global OEM/Integrators

Full-service automation providers go direct-to-market with their own products and complementary products via partnerships. They offer a full life cycle of services from design to implementation and aftermarket services. Larger providers have a global reach, while some focus on a regional geographic footprint.

Company	Headquarters	Geographic Focus	Industry Coverage
Daifuku	Japan	Global	Broad
Dematic	USA	Global	Broad
FORTNA	USA	Regional—NA	Broad
Honeywell Intelligrated	USA	Regional—NA	Broad
Knapp	Austria	Global	Broad
Murata	Japan	Regional—APAC	Targeted
SSI Schaefer Group	Germany	Global	Broad
Swisslog	Switzerland	Global	Broad
System Logistics	Italy	Regional—Europe	Targeted
TGW	Austria	Global	Broad
Vanderlande	The Netherlands	Global	Broad
Witron	Germany	Global	Targeted

Mid-Size Integrators

Full-service automation providers go direct-to-market with their own products and complementary products via partnerships. They offer a full life cycle of services from design, to implementation and aftermarket services. Many of these integrators focus on a specific geographic region and/ or limit the industry verticals they serve.

Company	Headquarters	Geographic Focus	Industry Coverage
Automha	Italy	Regional—Europe	Targeted
Bastian	USA	Regional—NA	Broad
Gebhardt	Germany	Regional—Europe	Targeted
Hy-tek	USA	Regional—NA	Broad
Korber	Germany	Regional—Europe	Targeted
Numina	USA	Regional—NA	Broad
Savoie	France	Regional—Europe	Targeted
Stocklin	Switzerland	Regional—Europe	Targeted
Symbotic	USA	Regional—NA	Targeted
Vargo	USA	Regional—NA	Targeted

Subsystem Providers: AGVs and AMRs

These providers focus on delivering pallet and/or tote transportation and storage solutions in the warehouse. They do this through a product line of Automated Guided Vehicles and Autonomous Mobile Robots.

Company	Headquarters	Geographic Focus
6 River Systems	USA	Global
Addverb	USA	Global
Agilox	Austria	Global
Balyo	France	Global
Electric 80	Italy	Global
Fetch (Zebra)	USA	Regional—NA
ForwardX	China	Regional—APAC
Geek +	China	Global

Grenzebach	Germany	Global
Grey Orange	USA	Global
Hai Robotics	China	Global
JBT	USA	Global
Locus Robotics	USA	Global
Mobile Industrial Robots (MiR)	Denmark	Global
Movu Robotics	Belgium	Regional—EMEA
Omron/Adept	Japan	Global
Onward Robotics	USA	Regional—NA
Otto Motors	Canada	Regional—NA
Quicktron	China	Global
Seegrid	USA	Regional—NA
Transbotics (Scott)	USA	Global
Tompkins	USA	Global
Vecna	USA	Regional—NA

Subsystem Providers: ASRS Storage

These providers focus on delivering storage solutions in the warehouse. They do this through a product line of Unit Load or Mini Load cranes or Vertical Lift Modules.

Company	Headquarters	Geographic Focus
Dambach	Germany	Regional—Europe
Interlake Mecalux	Spain	Regional—Europe
Kardex	Switzerland	Global
Modula	USA	Global
Murata	Japan	Regional—APAC
Viastore	Germany	Regional—Europe

Subsystem Providers: ASRS Picking

These providers focus on delivering storage-based picking solutions in the warehouse. They do this through a product line of shuttle or robot on grid subsystems.

Company	Headquarters	Geographic Focus
Attabotics	Canada	Regional—NA
AutoStore	Norway	Global
Brightpick	USA	Regional—NA
Exotec	France	Regional—Europe
Ocado	UK	Global
OPEX	USA	Global
Reel-in Robotics	Canada	Regional—NA

Subsystem Providers: Convey-Sort

These providers focus on delivering transportation and sortation solutions in the warehouse. They do this through broad conveyor product lines and high-speed sortation technologies.

Company	Headquarters	Geographic Focus
Beumer Group	Germany	Global
Eurosort	The Netherlands	Global
Ferag	Switzerland	Regional—Europe
Fives Intralogistics	France	Regional—Europe
Hytrol	USA	Regional—NA
Intralox	USA	Global
SDI	USA	Regional—NA
Siemens Logistics	Germany	Global

Pureplay Technology Providers: Robotics

These providers focus on delivering robotics solutions in the warehouse. They do this primarily through a combination of software, multi-axis robotics, vision, and end effectors. At this time, these technology providers all operate in targeted industries.

Company	Headquarters	Geographic Focus
Ambi	USA	Regional—NA
Berkshire Grey	USA	Regional—NA
Covariant	USA	Regional—NA

Dexterity	USA	Regional—NA
Hikrobot	China	Regional—APAC
Kindred	Canada	Regional—NA
Mujin	Japan	Regional—APAC
Osaro	USA	Regional—NA
Photoneo	Slovakia	Regional—Europe
Plus One Robotics	USA	Regional—NA
Right Hand Robotics	USA	Regional—NA

Pureplay Technology Providers WMS/WES

These providers focus on software solutions for the warehouse. Several provide a broader, enterprise focus, while others provide a focus on processing within the four walls of the warehouse, integrating with material handling equipment.

Company	Headquarters	Geographic Focus
Ascent	USA	Regional—NA
Blue Yonder	USA	Global
Manhattan	USA	Global
Matthews Automation	USA	Regional—NA
Oracle	USA	Global
SAP	Germany	Global
Softeon	USA	Global

Appendix 2: Acronyms

Acronym	Stands for
3PL	Third Party Logistics
AFE	Amazon Fulfillment Engine
AGC	Automated Guided Cart
AGV	Automated Guided Vehicle
AI	Artificial Intelligence
AMR	Autonomous Mobile Robot
ASN	Advanced Shipment Notice
API	Application Programming Interface
ARB	Activated Roller Belt
ASRS	Automated Storage and Retrieval System
ATLS	Automated Truck Loading System
BDLR	Belt-Driven Live Roller
BI	Business Intelligence
BOL	Bill of Lading
CAGR	Compound Annual Growth Rate
CDLR	Chain Driven Live Roller
CMMS	Computerized Maintenance Management System
DC	Distribution Center
DW	Data Warehouse
EDI	Electronic Data Interchange
ERP	Enterprise Resource Planning
FaaS	Fulfillment-as-a-Service
FC	Fulfillment Center
FCL	Full Container Load
FIFO	First In First Out
FTL	Full Truck Load
GDP	Gross Domestic Product
GTP	Goods-to-Person
GTR	Goods-to-Robot
IBC	Intermediate Bulk Container
IoT	Internet of Things
LiDAR	Light Detection and Ranging
LIFO	Last In First Out
LPA	Label, Print, and Apply

Acronym	Stands for
LPN	License Plate Number
LTL	Less than Load
MFC	Micro-Fulfillment Center
ML	Machine Learning
MPB	Modular Plastic Belted
MRP	Manufacturing Resource Planning
NRF	National Retail Federation
PLC	Programmable Logic Controller
PTG	Person-to-Goods
QR	Quick Response (code)
RaaS	Robot-as-a-Service
RAT	Right Angle Transfer
RF	Radio Frequency
REST	Representational State Transfer
RFID	Radio Frequency Identification
RMA	Return Merchandise Authorization
ROI	Return on Investment
ROS	Robot Operating System
RPC	Remote Procedure Call
RTG	Robot-to-Goods
SaaS	Software-as-a-Service
SCM	Supply Chain Management
SKU	Stock Keeping Unit
SLA	Service Level Agreement
SLAM	Simultaneous Localization and Mapping
SLAM	Scan Label Apply Manifest
SMS	Short Messaging Service
TMS	Transportation Management System
VAS	Value Added Services
VLM	Vertical Lift Module
VNA	Very Narrow Aisle
WCS	Warehouse Control System
WES	Warehouse Execution System
WMS	Warehouse Management System
YMS	Yard Management System

About the Authors

Peter Devenyi spent his 40-year engineering career working in software and technology development in the fields of networking, telecommunications, and logistics. He held senior executive positions at large global companies like RIM (BlackBerry) and Dematic. He earned bachelor's and master's degrees in Electrical Engineering from the University of Toronto. Currently, he consults in the field of Warehouse Automation and Logistics and teaches engineering leadership at the University of Toronto.

Dr. Miguel Pinilla has over 30 years' experience in the supply chain information systems industry. He held leadership positions at Dematic, RedPrairie (now Blue Yonder), SmartTurn, and Navis. Originally from Spain, he obtained a Senior Engineer Degree in Industrial Engineering from ICAI and came to the United States as a Fulbright scholar, obtaining a Masters in Engineering degree from Carnegie Mellon and a PhD from Stanford in Manufacturing Information Systems. Currently, he is principal of Salduba Technologies, advising clients in the field of Supply Chain Automation.

Jim Stollberg has business experience spanning over 35 years. He held senior executive roles in the automation and management consulting industries, including leadership positions with Dematic, HK Systems, and Accenture. He has participated in several successful equity transactions and continues to advise market-leading companies and thought leaders in the field of supply chain technology. He earned his bachelor's degree in Mechanical Engineering from Marquette University, where he also serves as Executive in Residence and as a member of the Supply Chain & Operations Management Advisory Board.

Index

www.ingramcontent.com/pod-product-compliance
Lightning Source LLC
Chambersburg PA
CBHW061306220326
41599CB00026B/4751